Geometric Nature Mandalas: 50 Unique Designs for All Ages to Color

Kayla M. Worley

Copyright © 2017 Kayla M. Worley

All rights reserved.

ISBN: 978-1976376061
ISBN-10: 1976376068

DEDICATION

Thank you to all of my friends and family who have supported my art over the years; fostering creativity brings a sense of relief and rejuvenation to one's spirit, and I am very grateful to share my own artistic endeavors with you all.

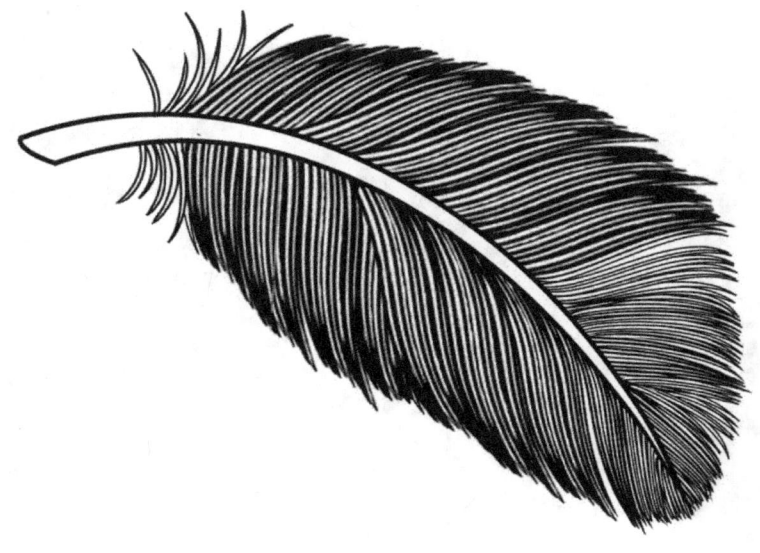

This book has been colored by:

_____

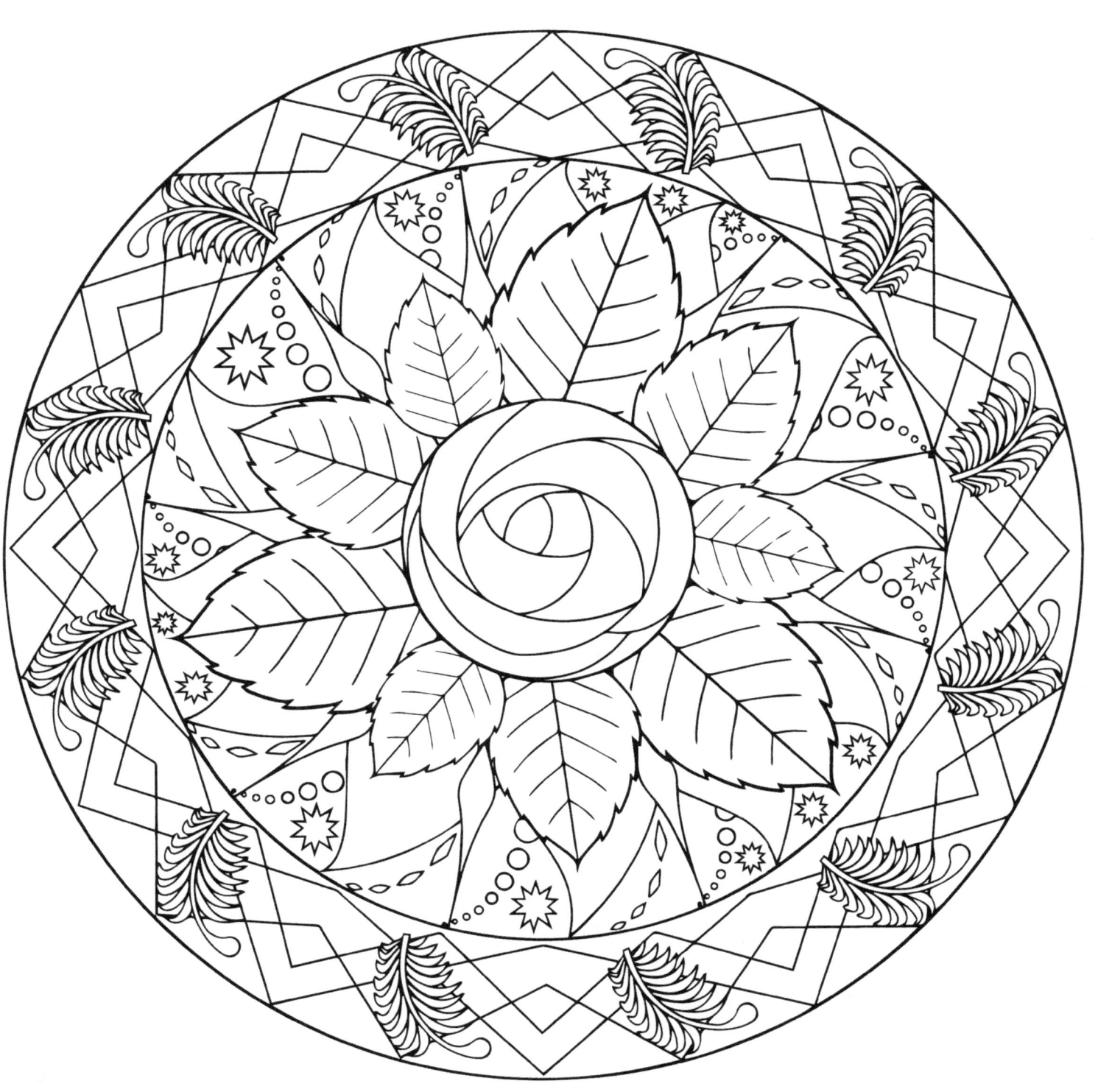

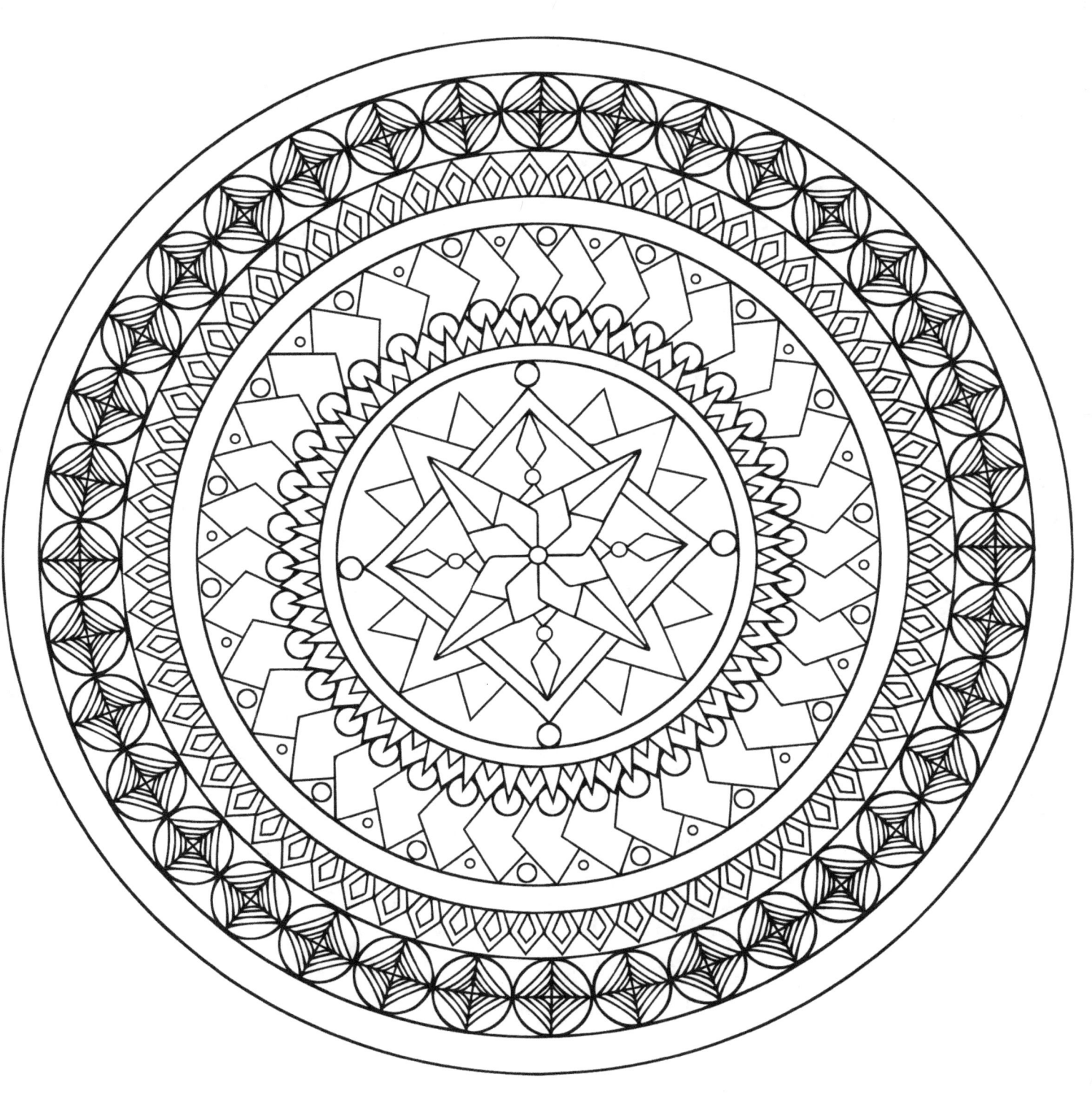

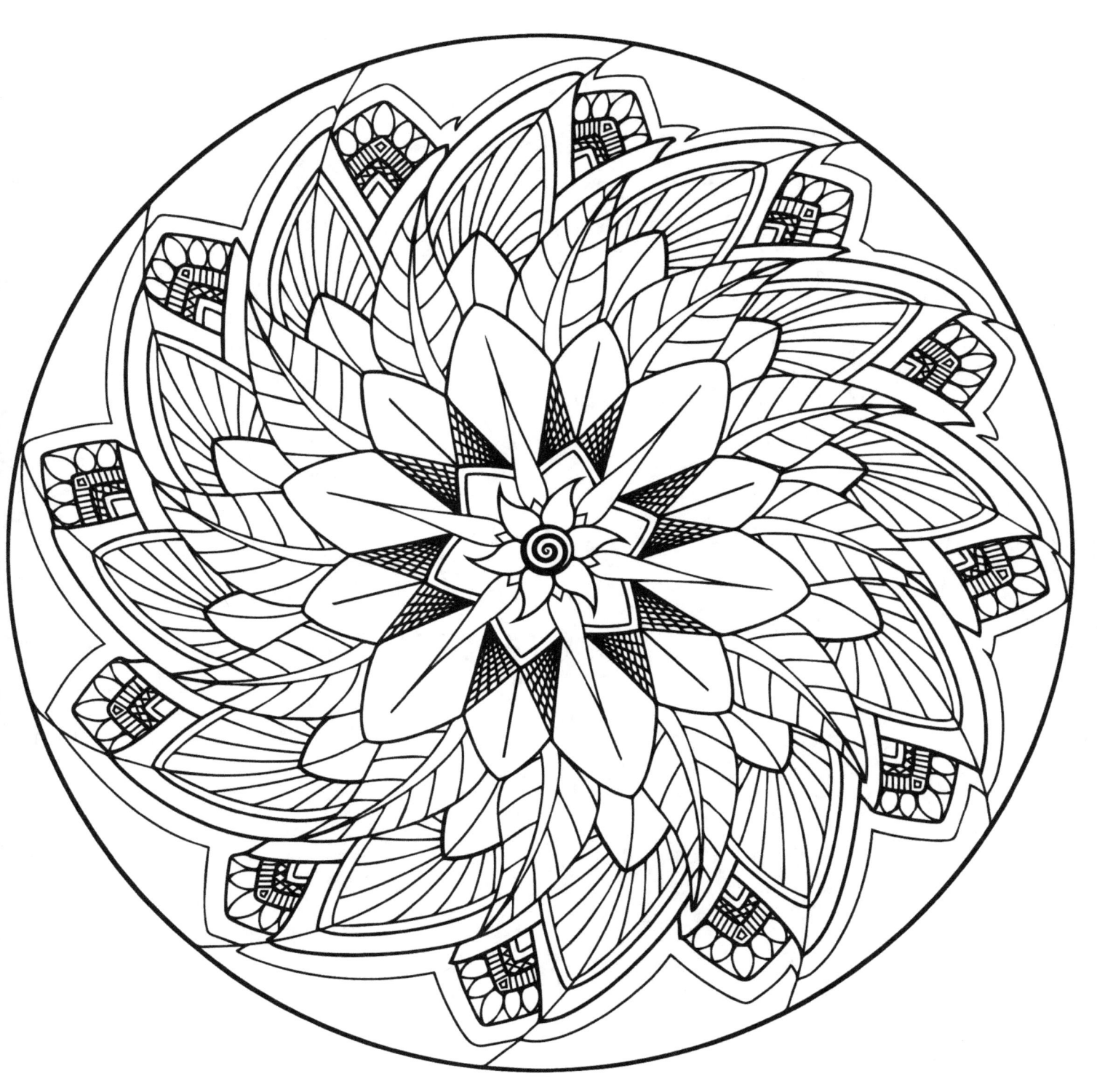

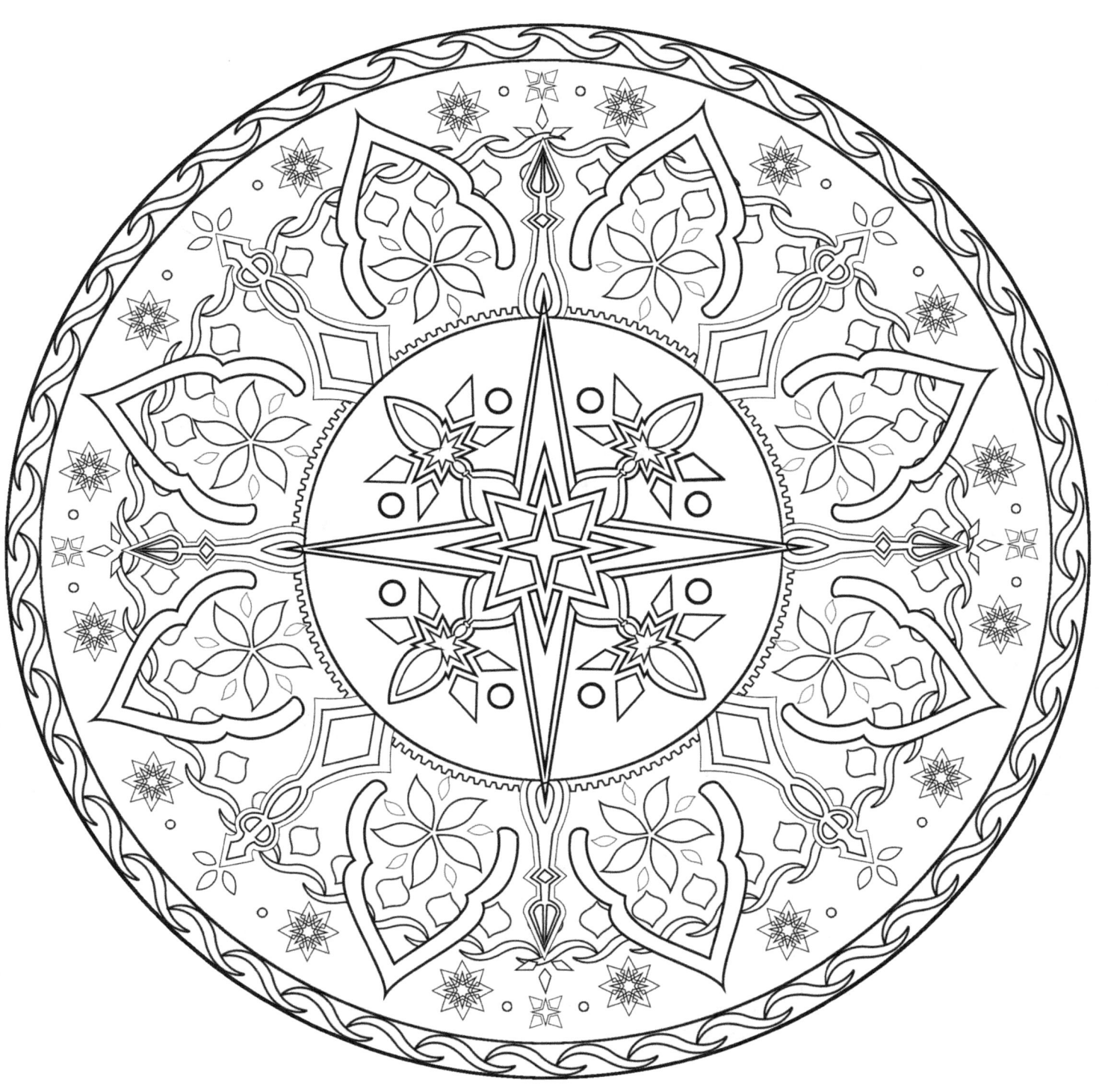

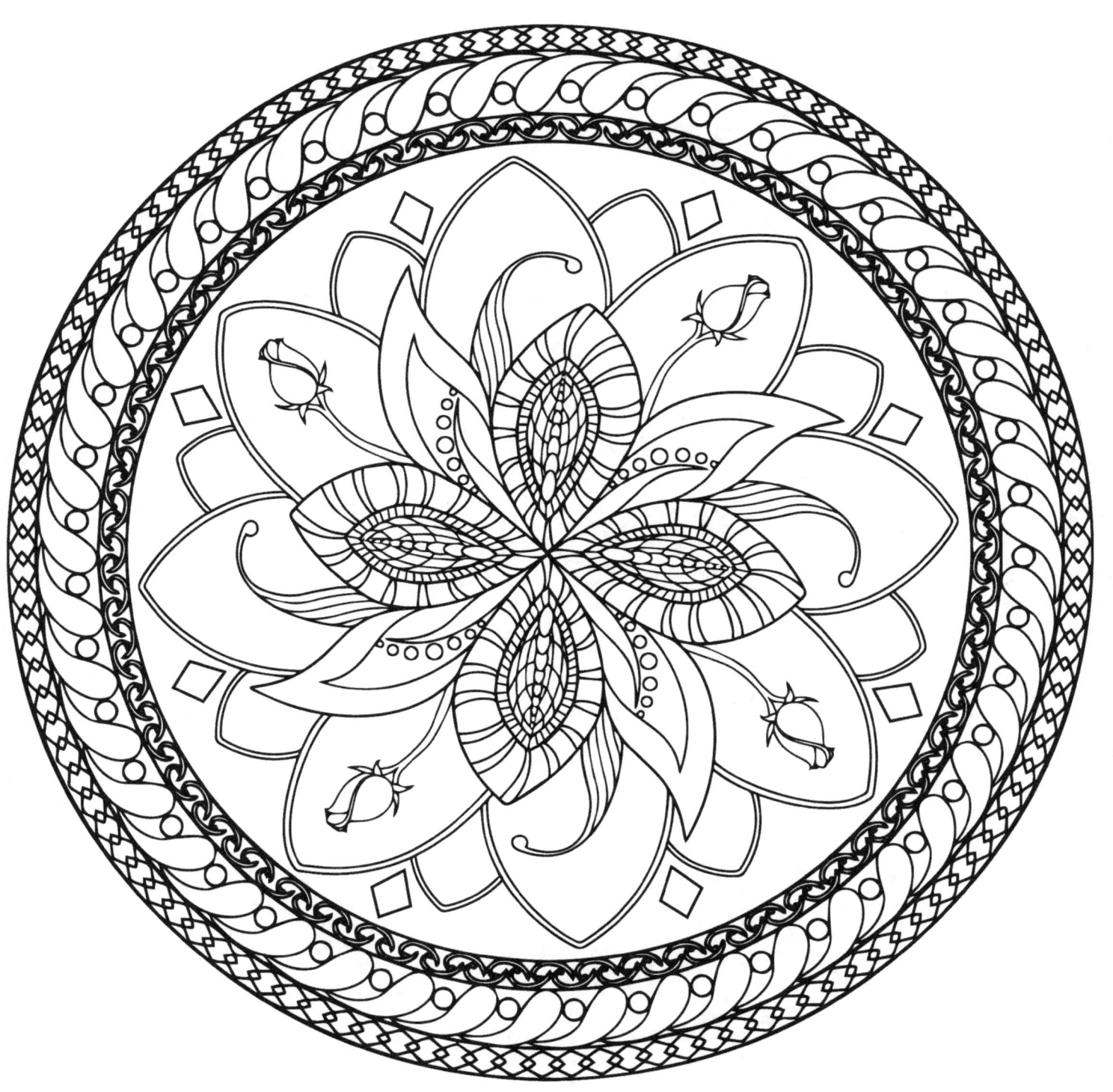

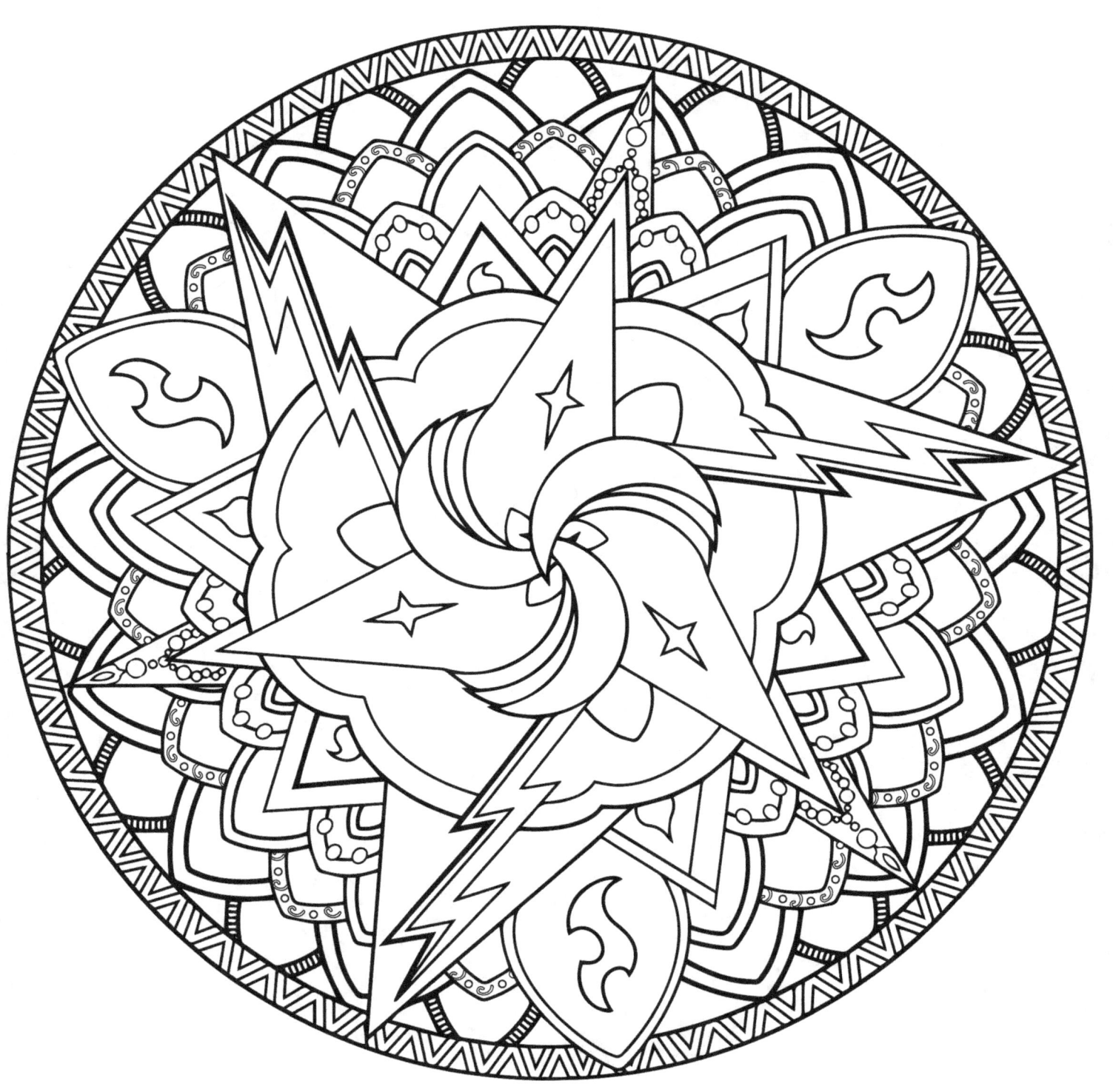

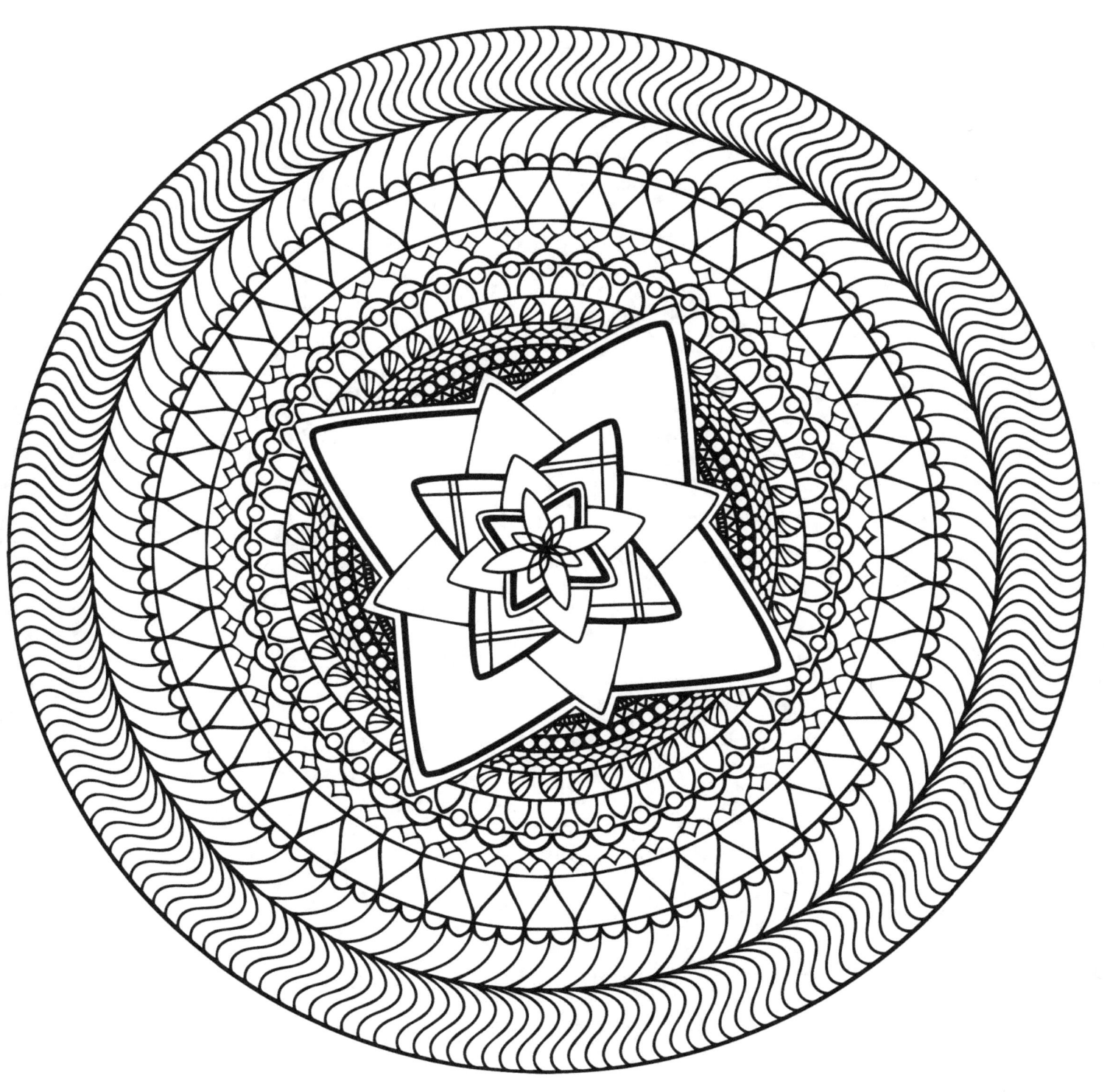

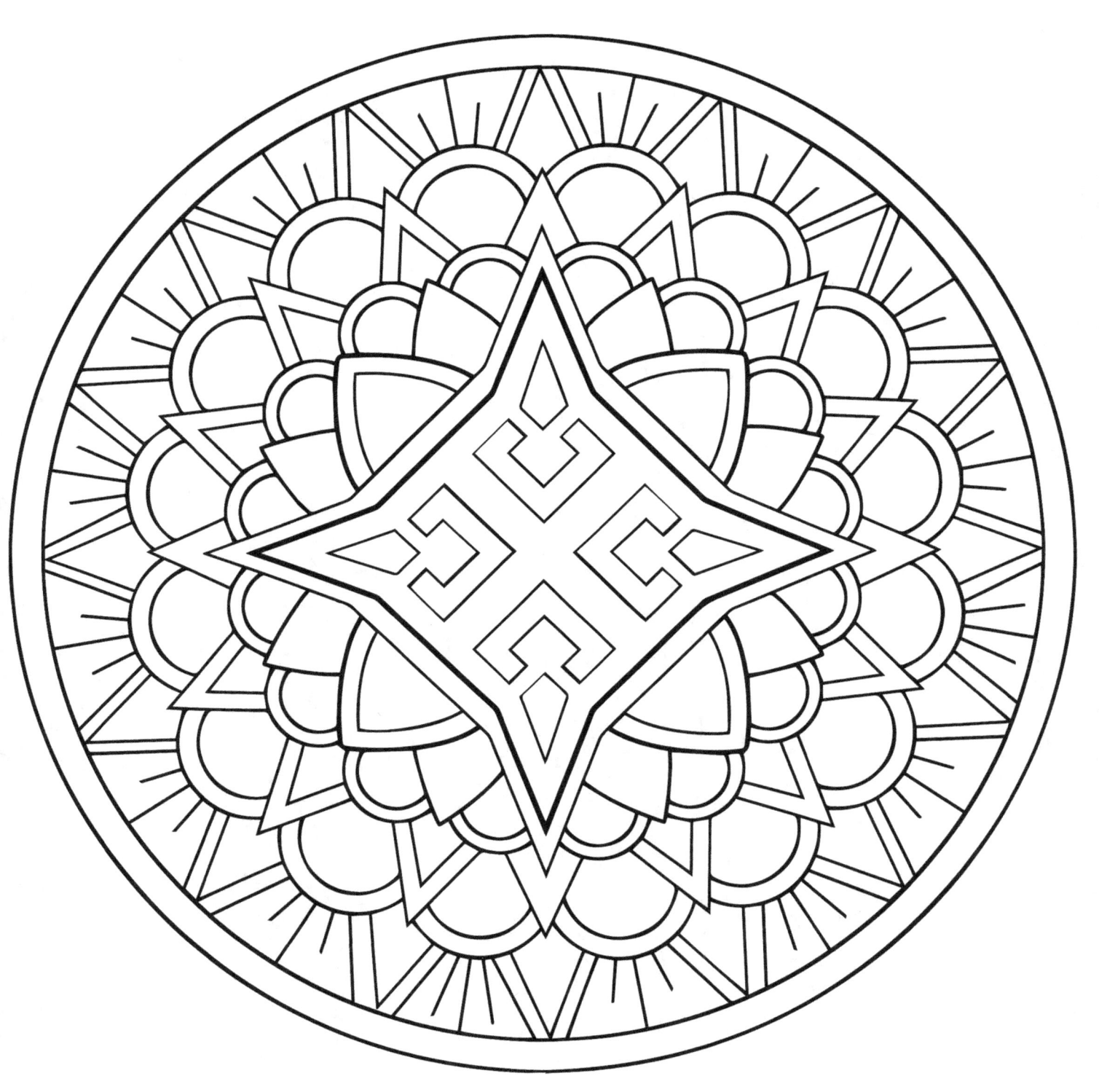

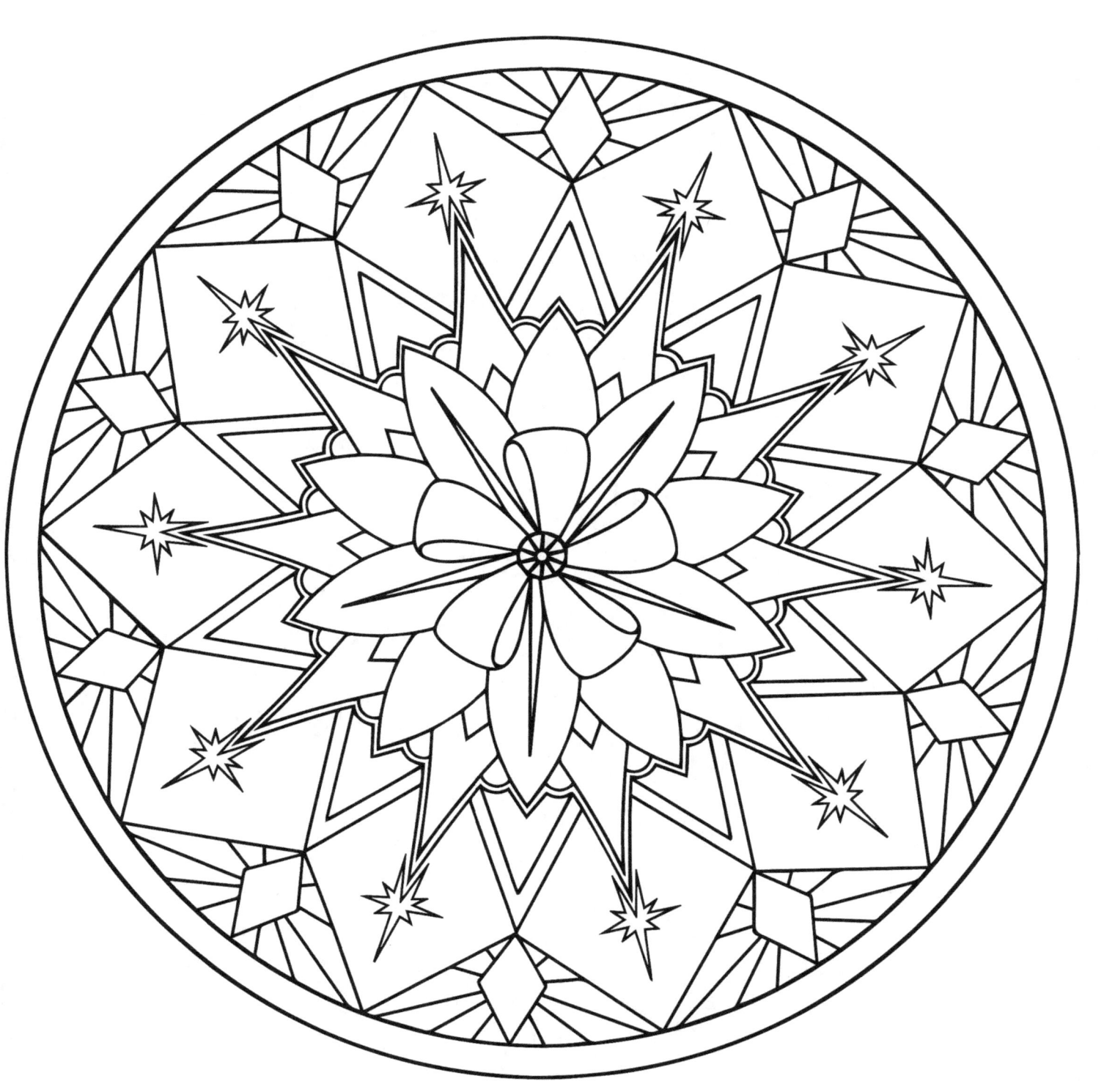

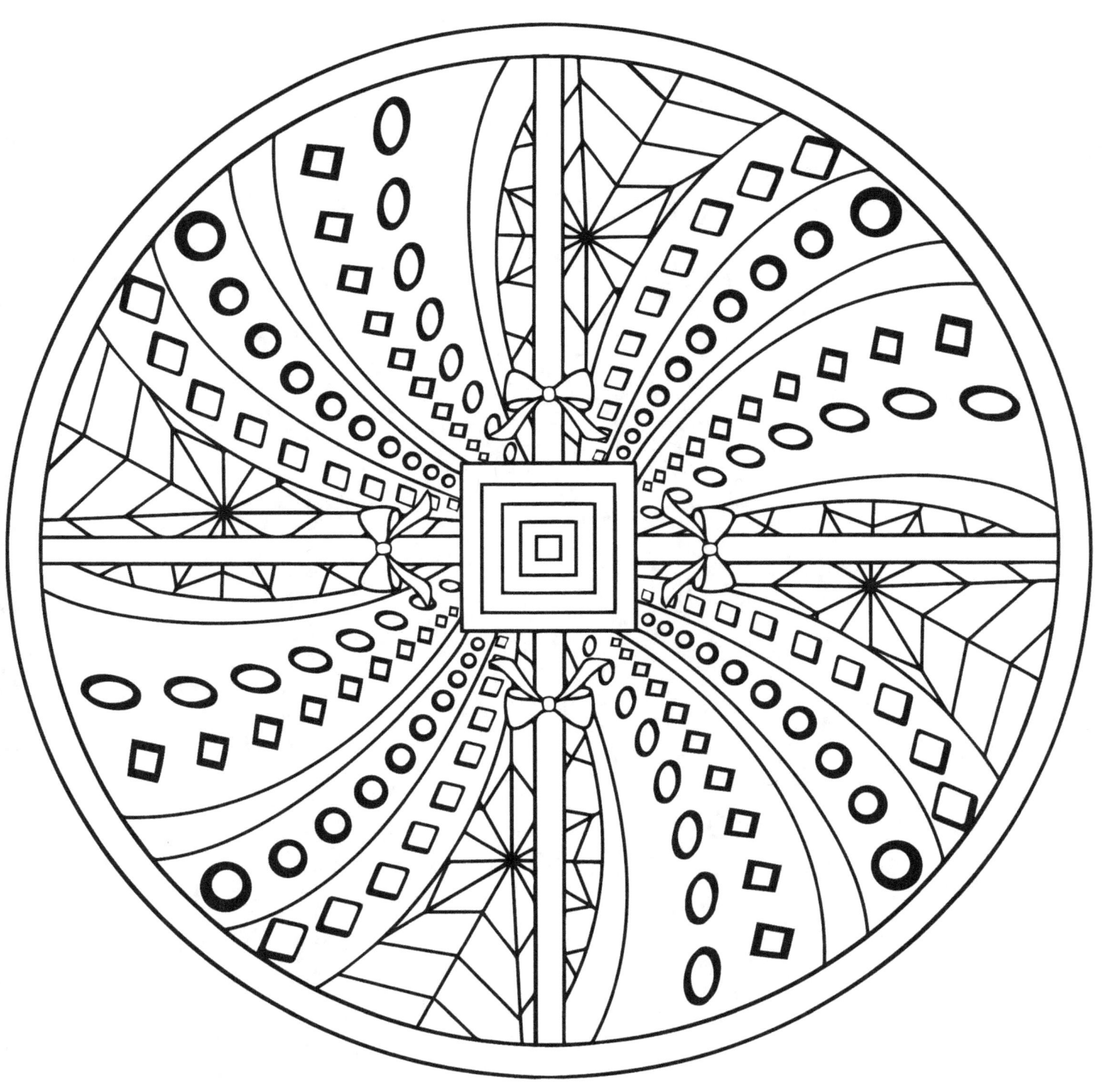

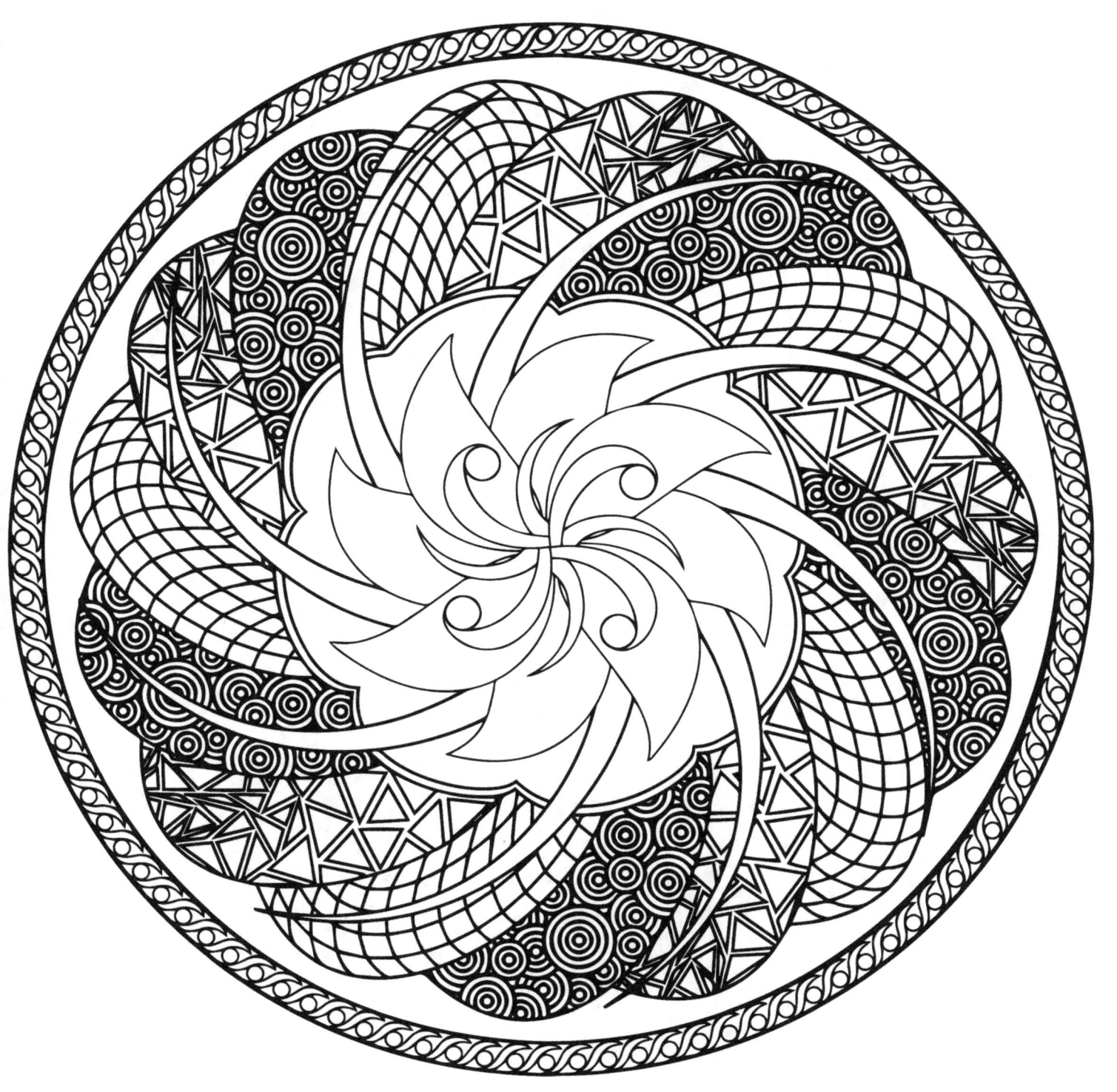

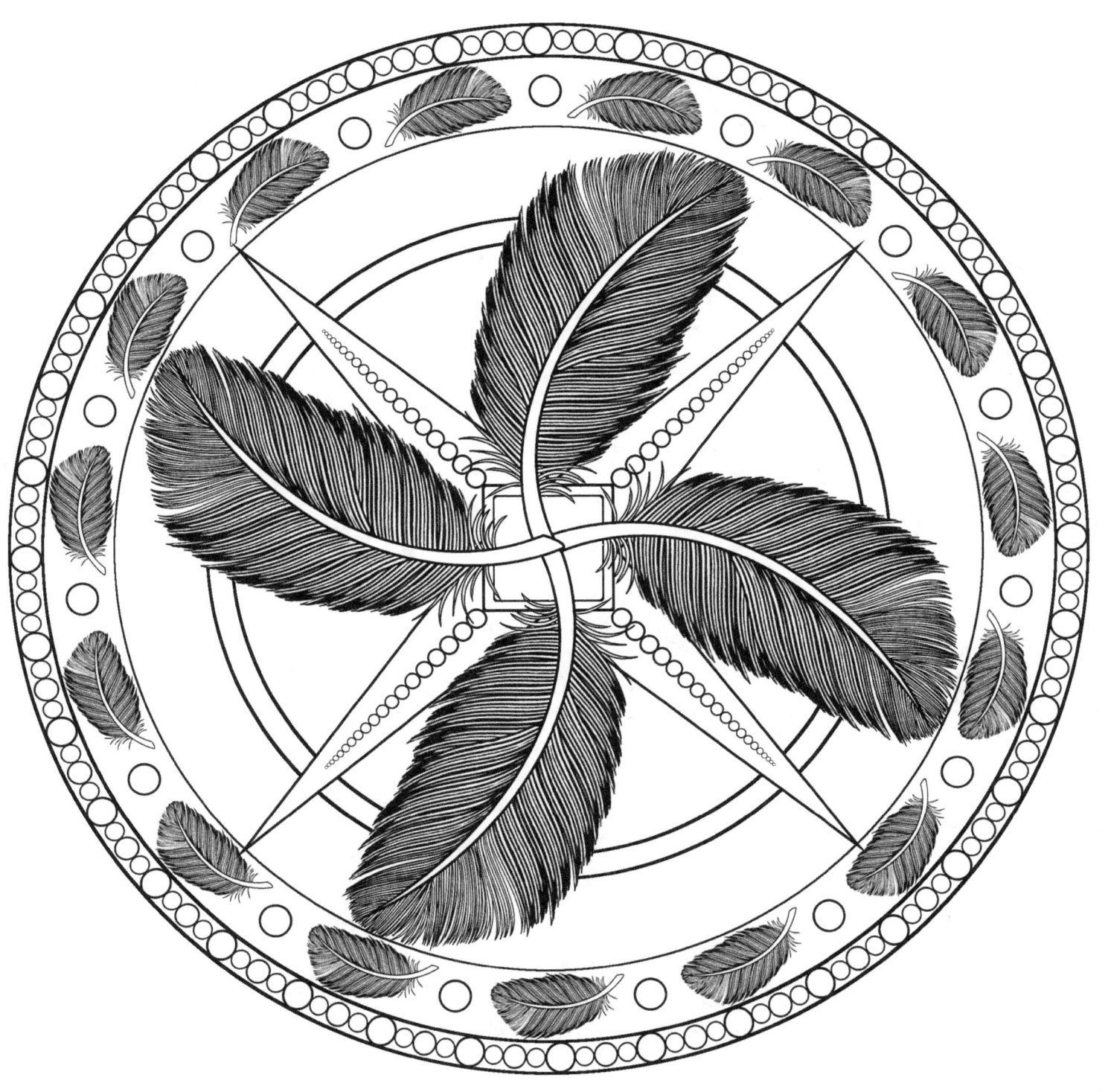

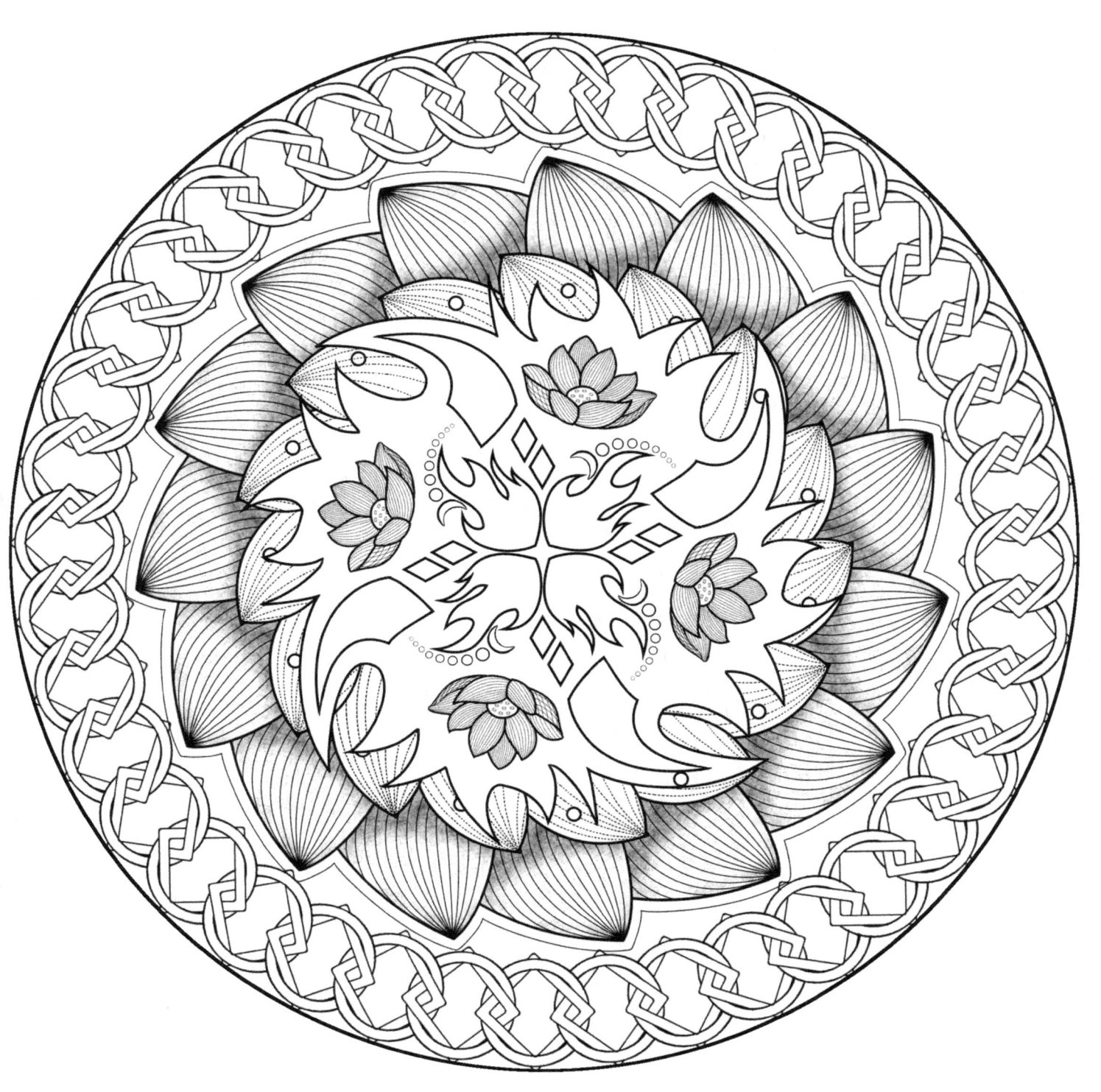

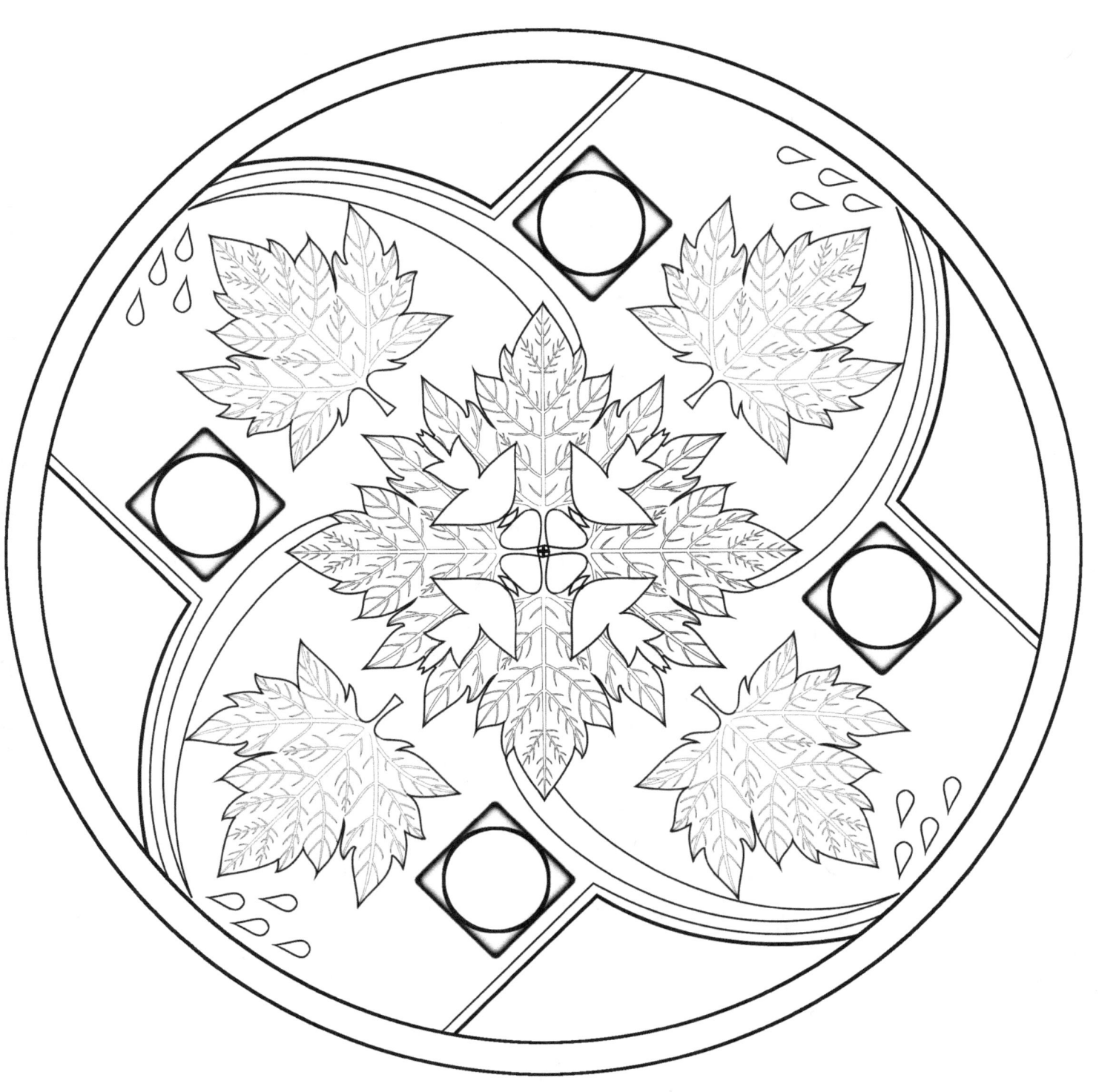

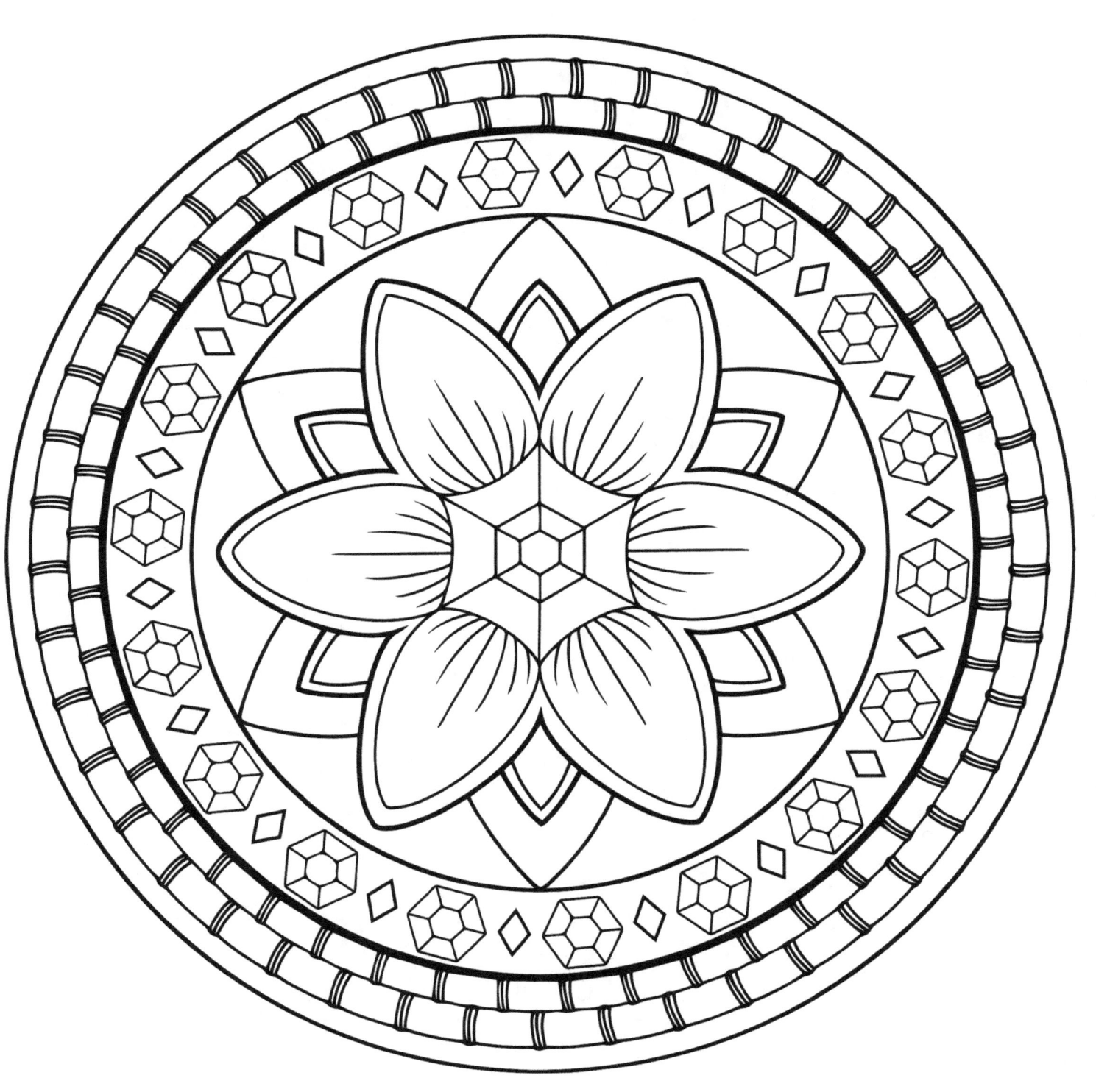

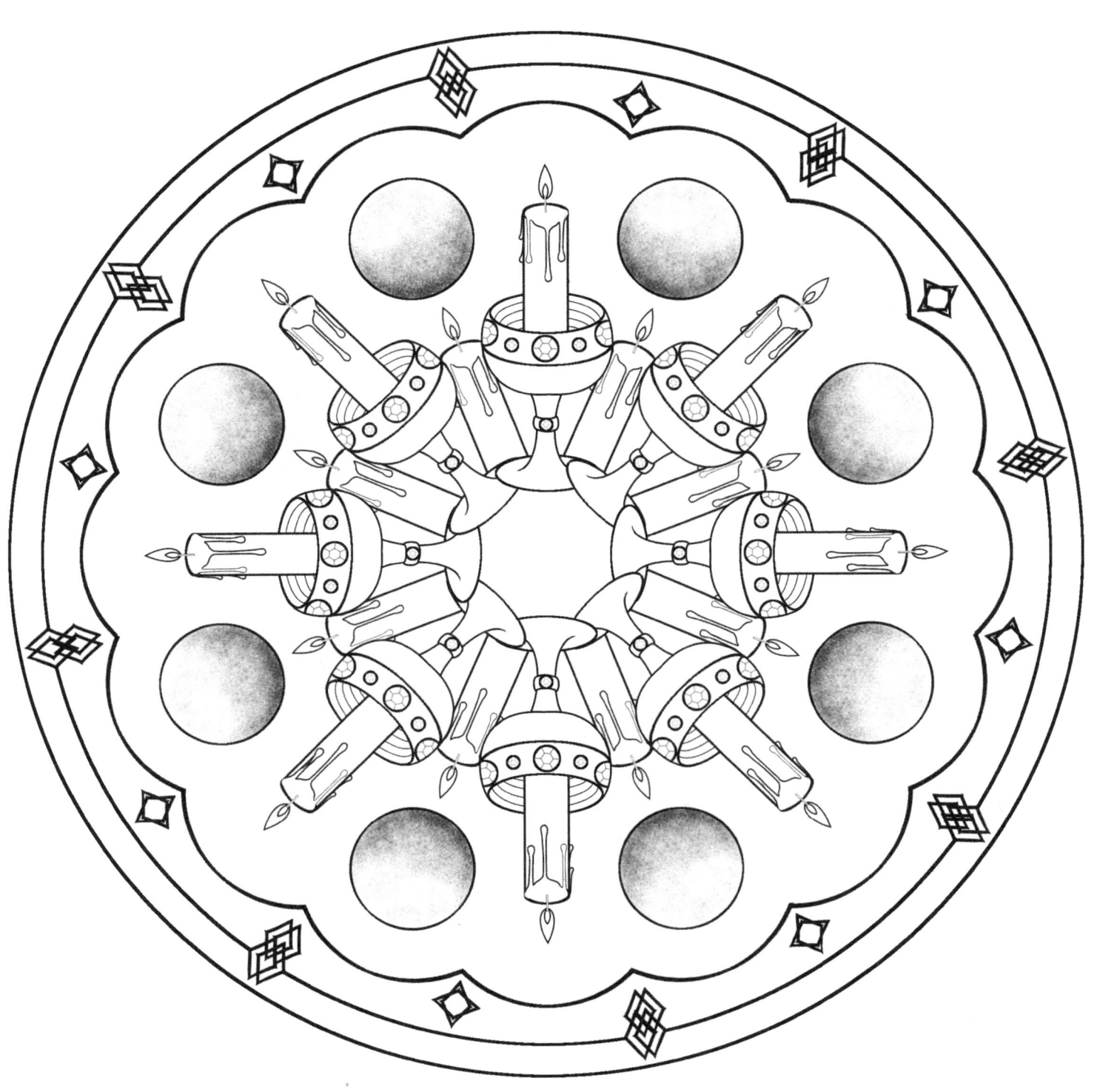

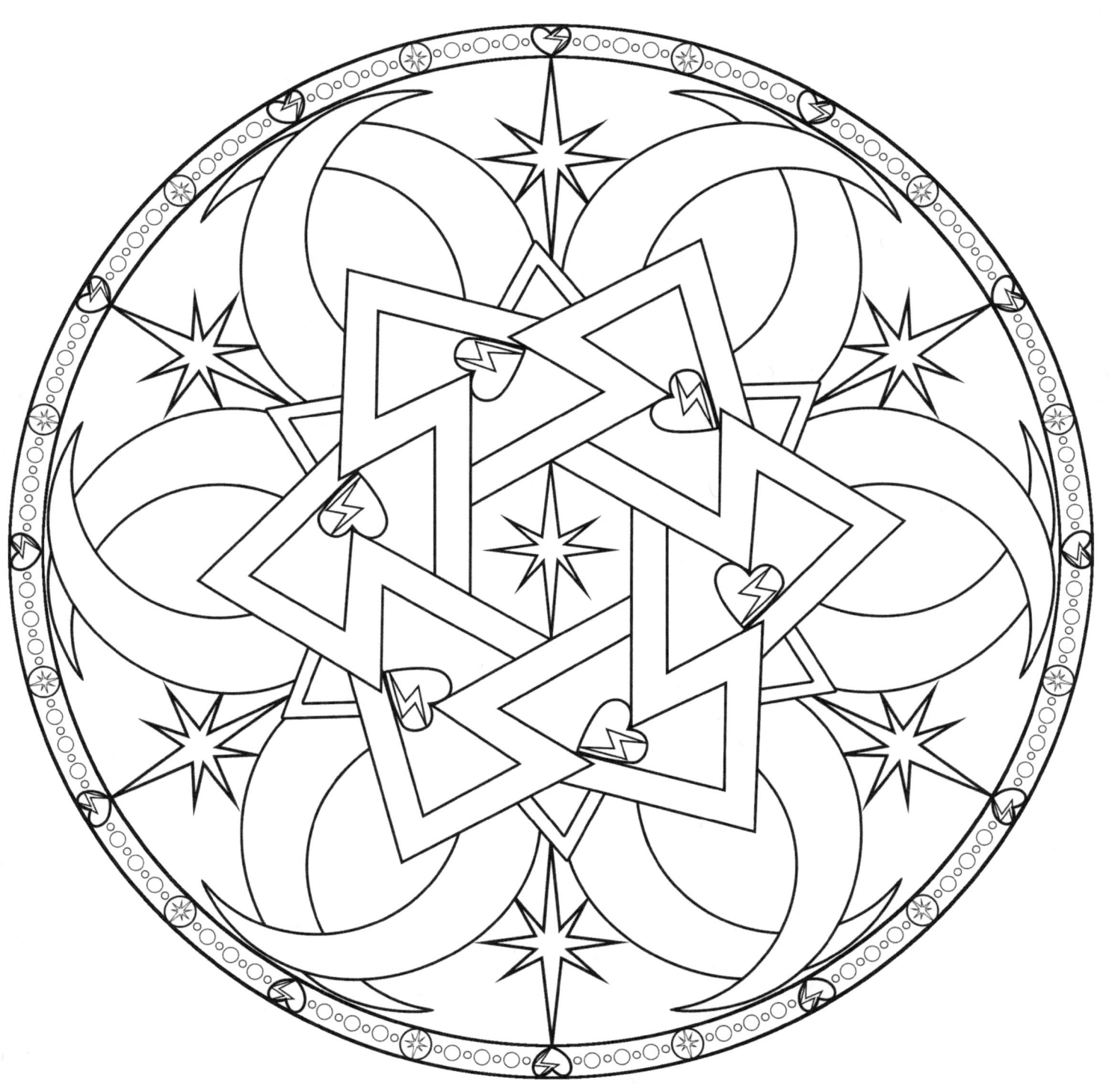

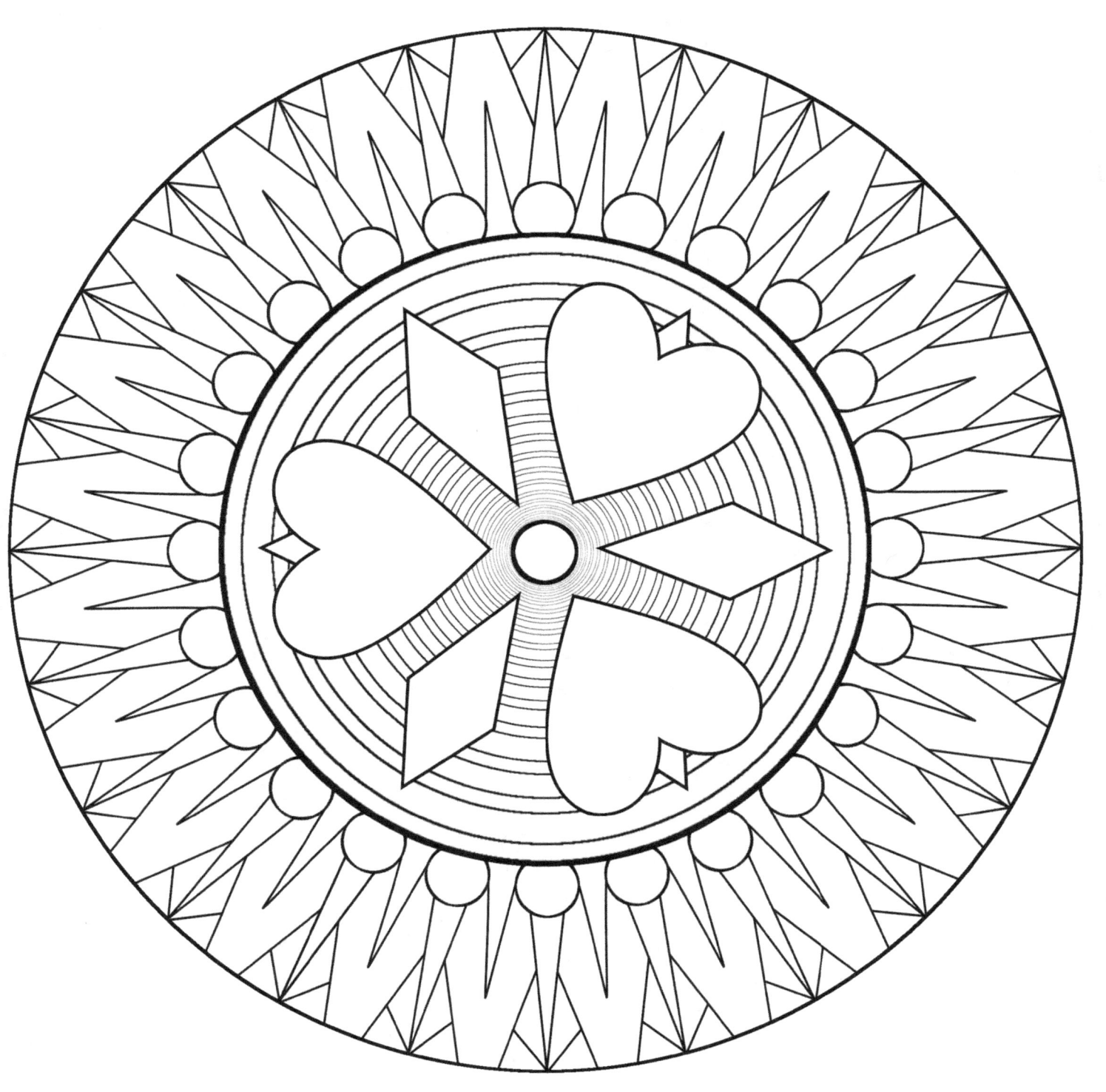

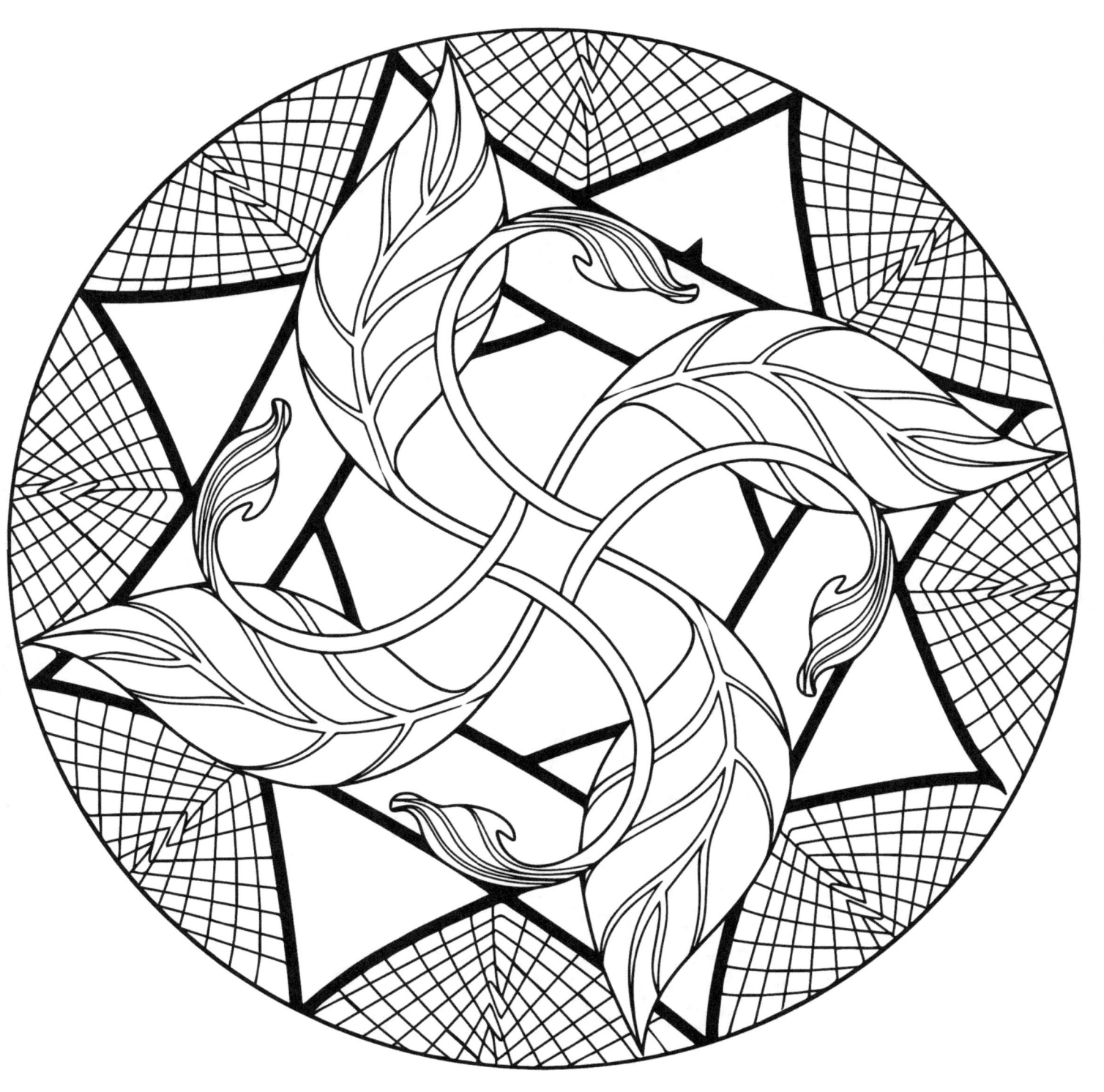

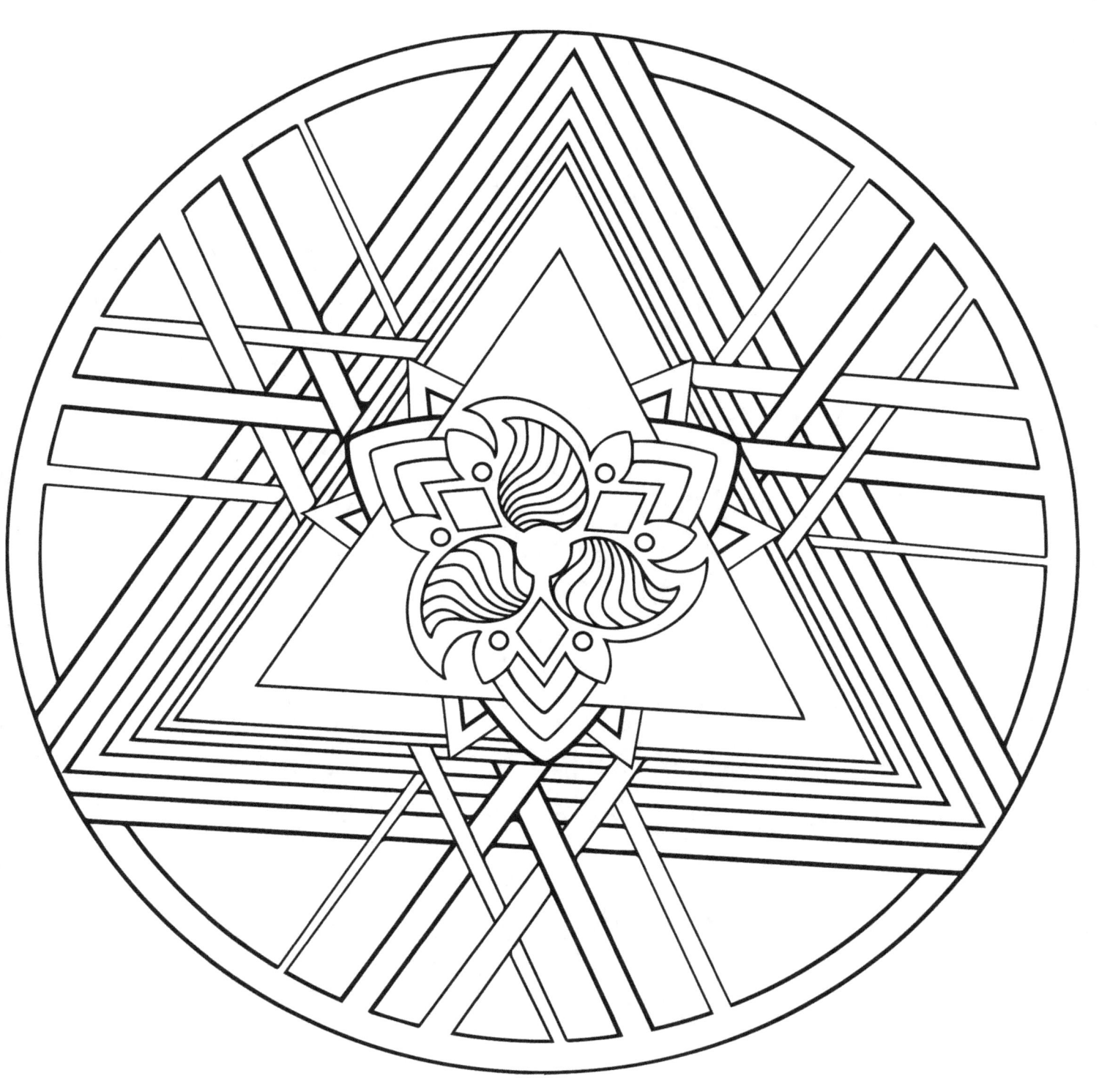

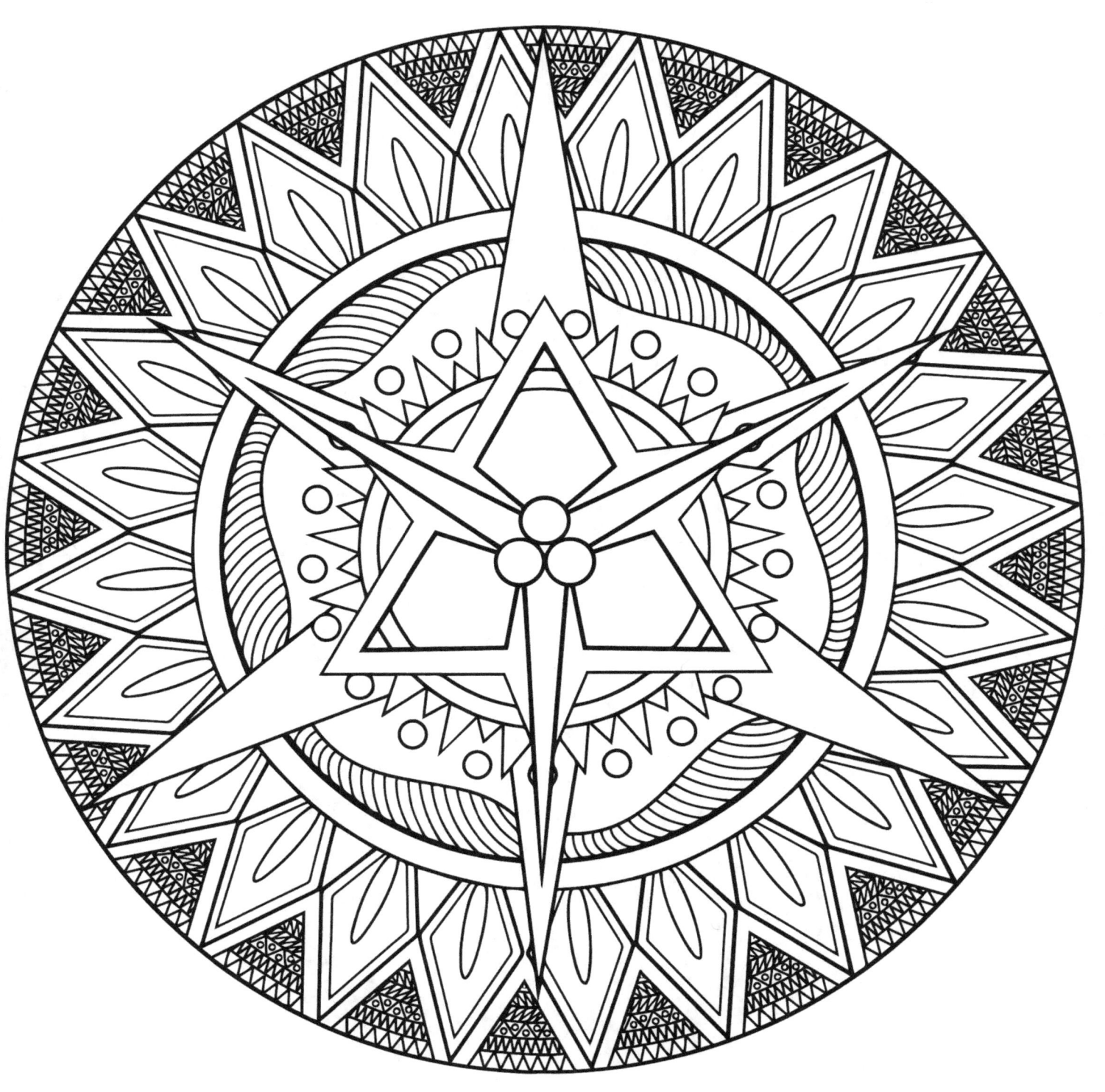

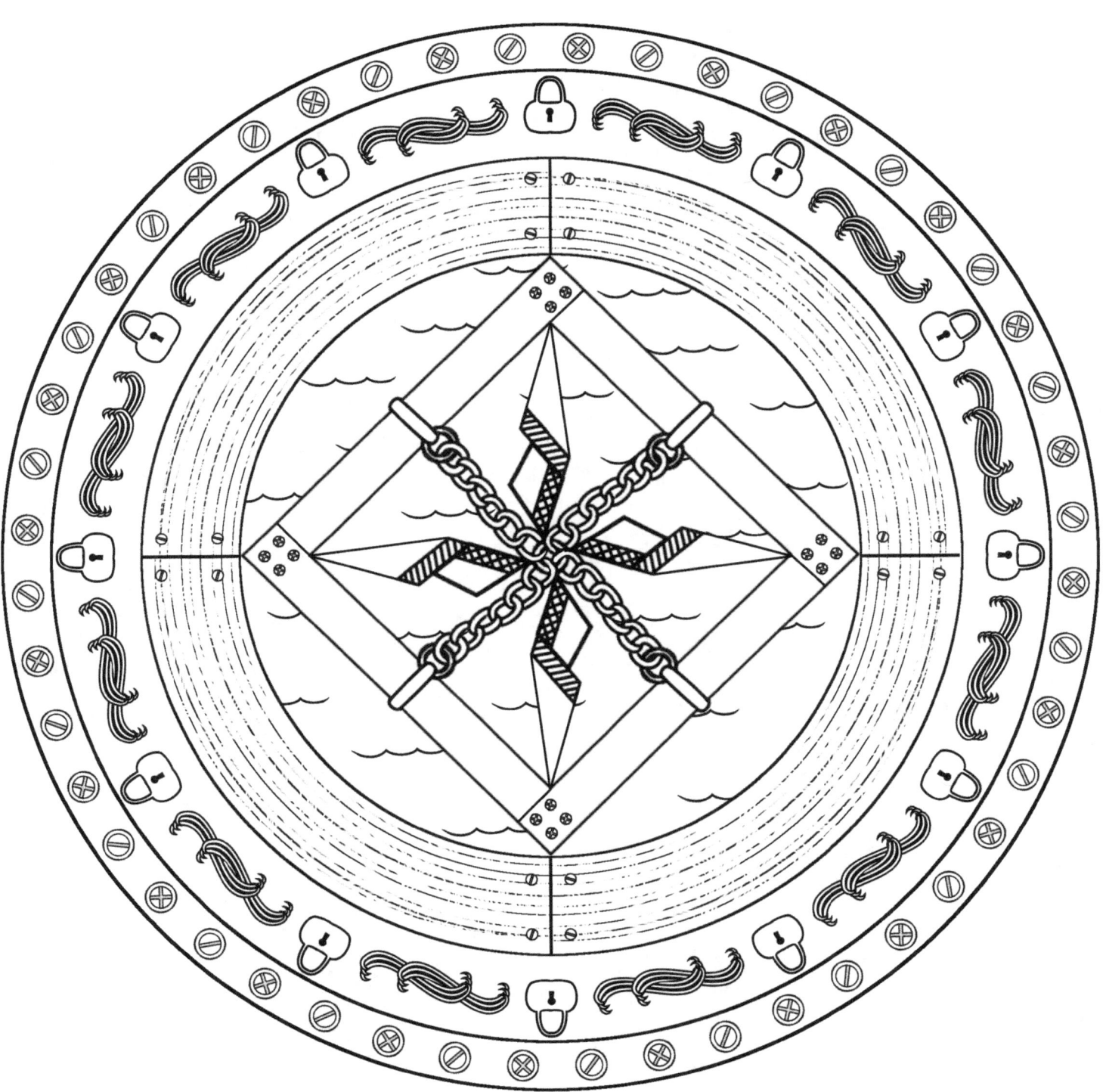

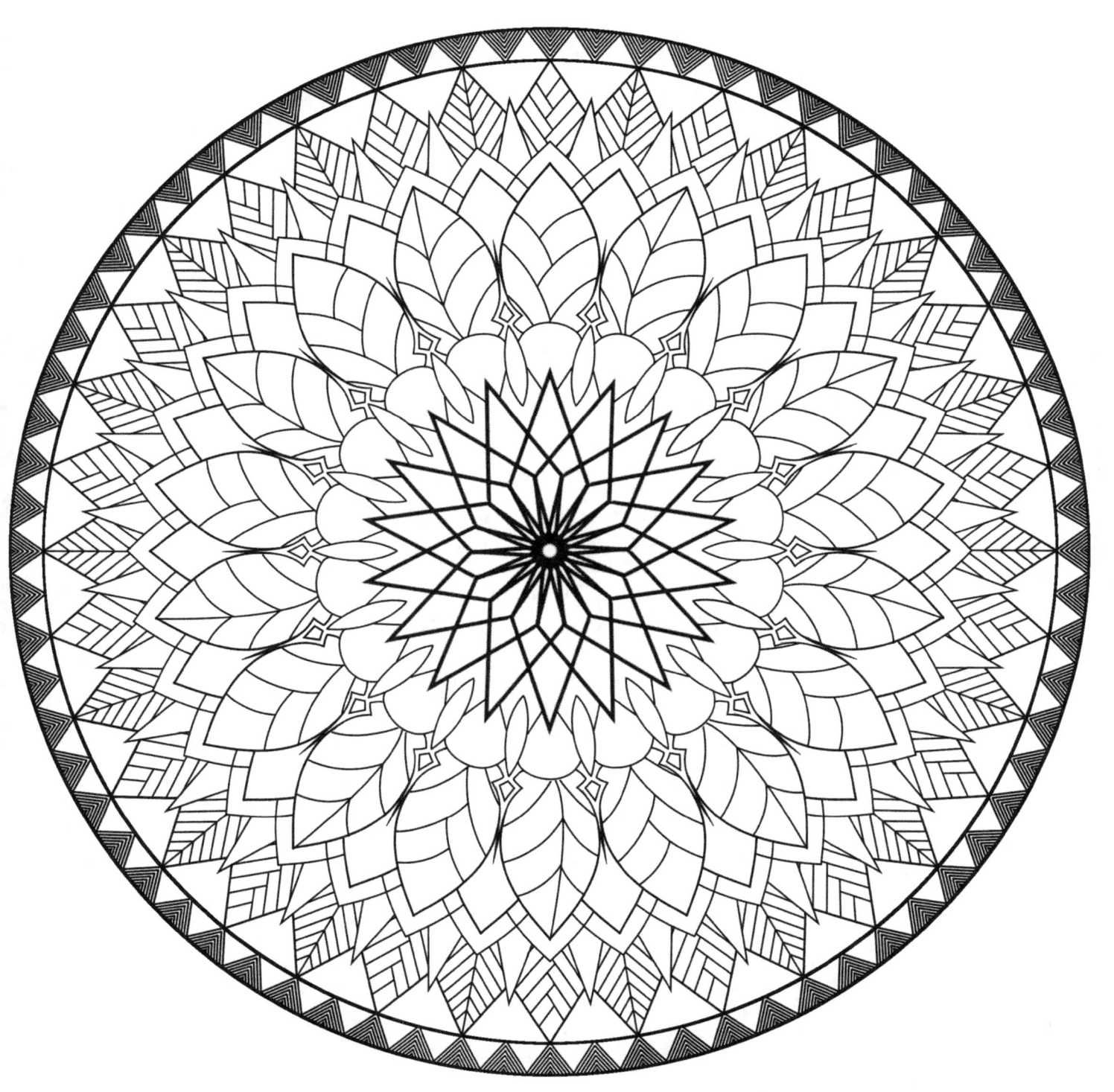

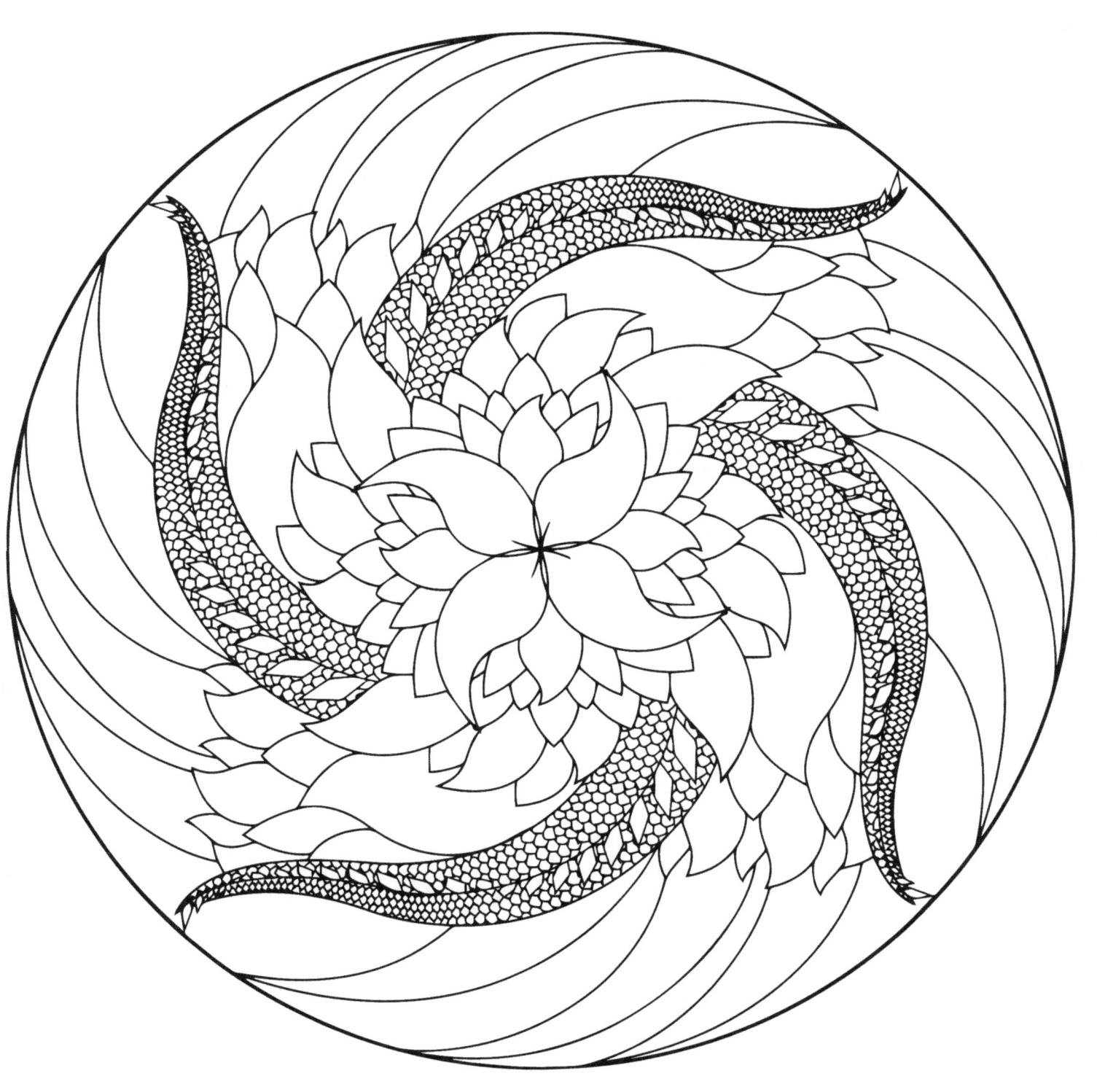

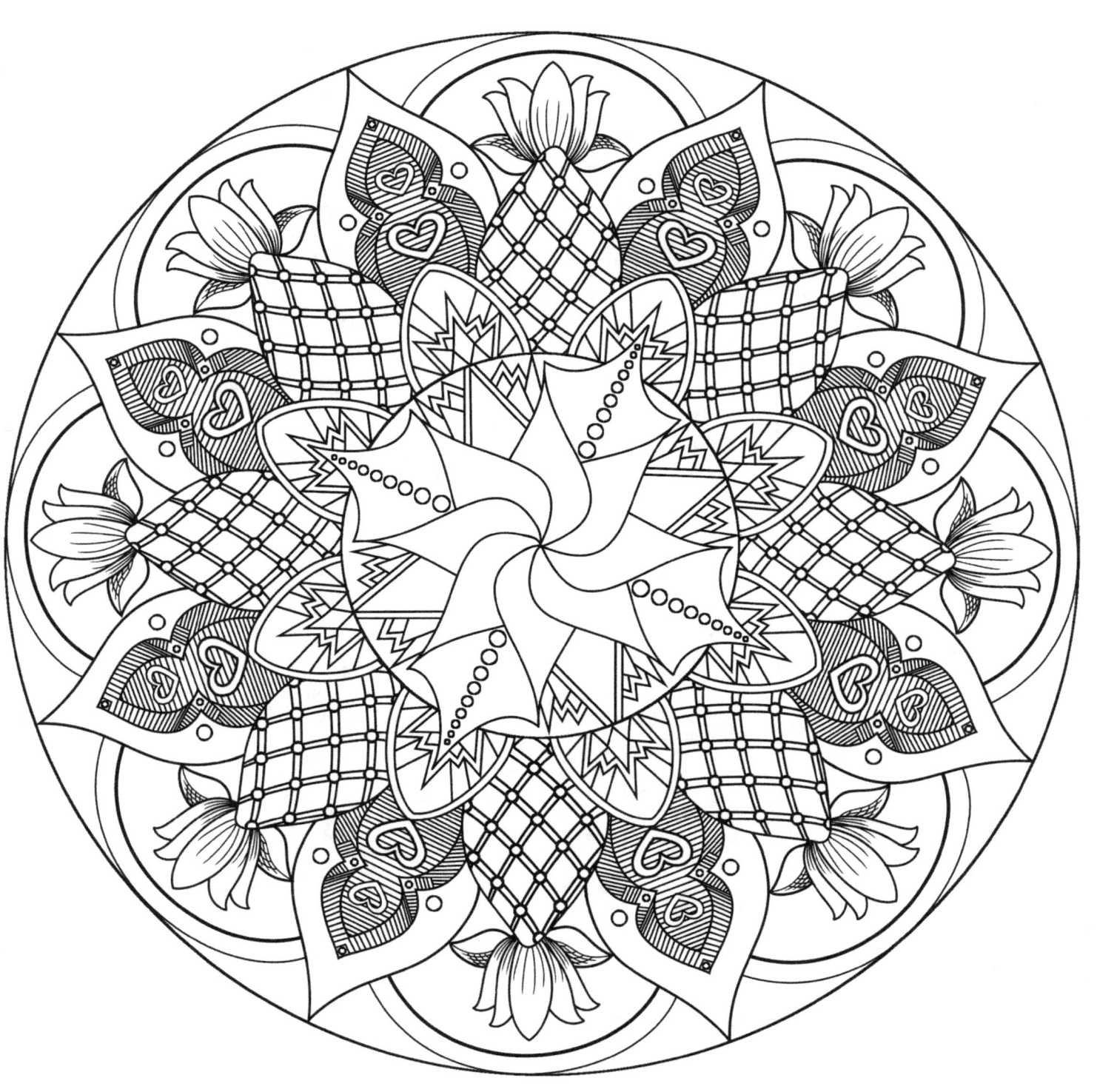

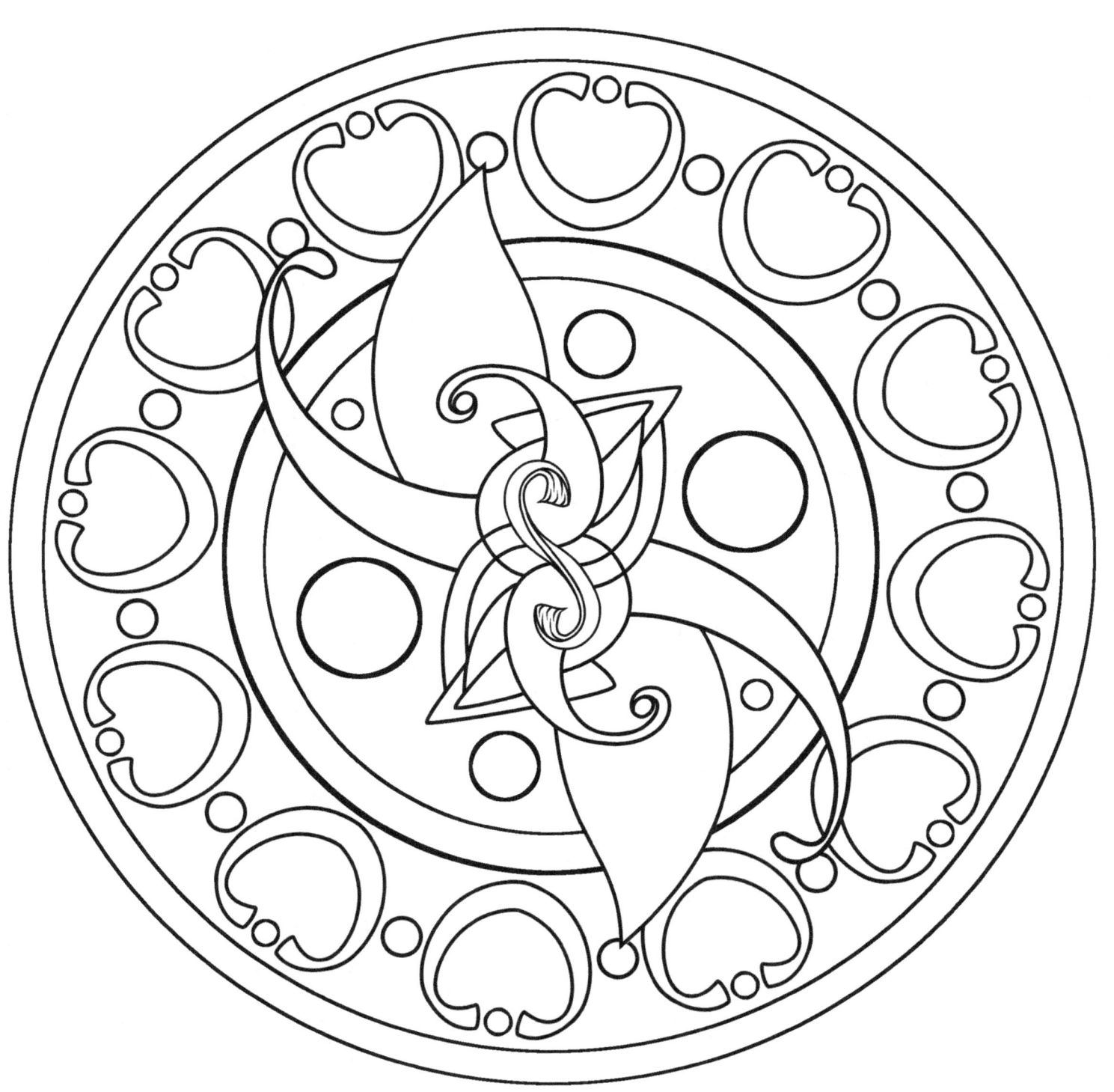

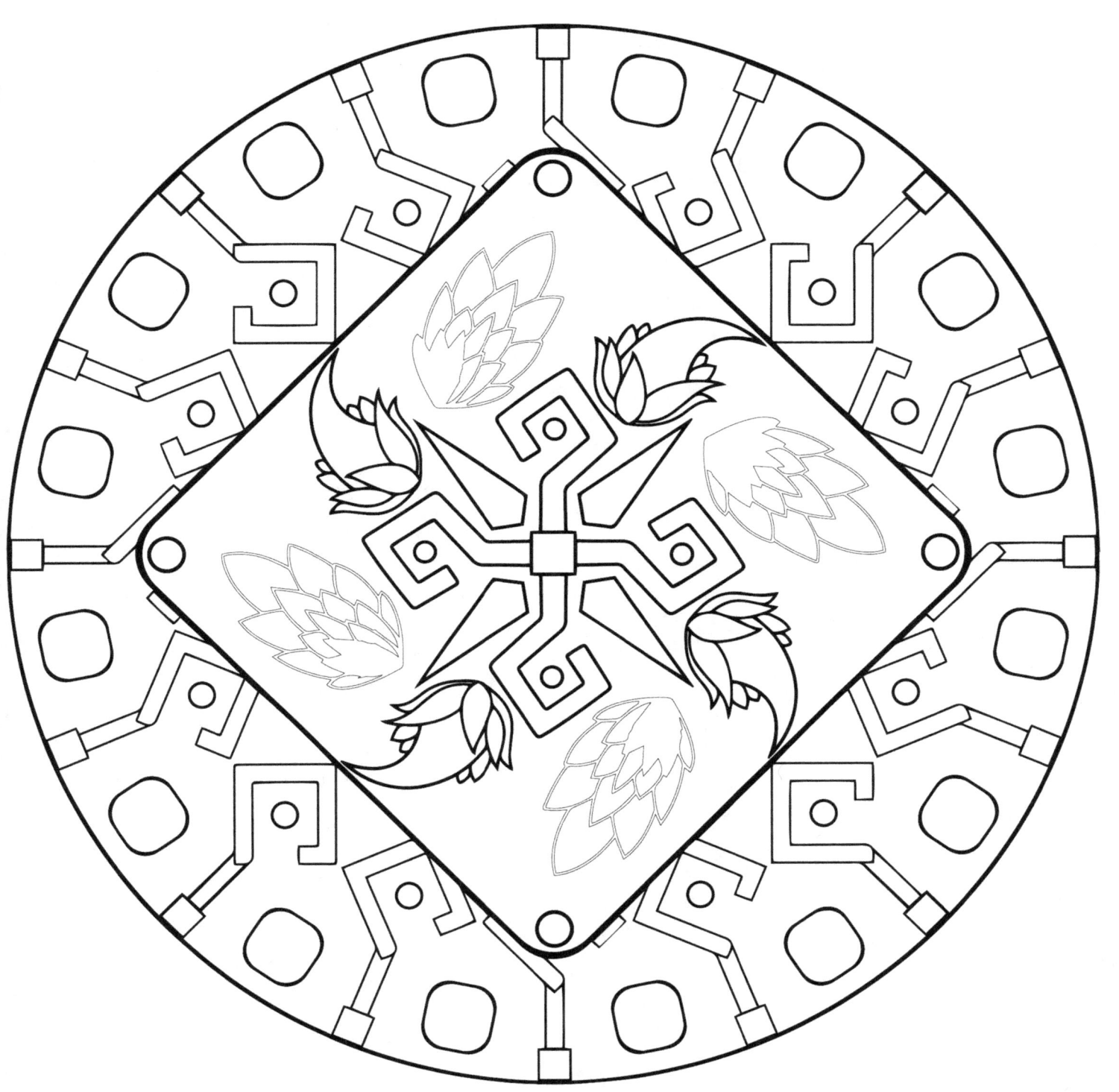

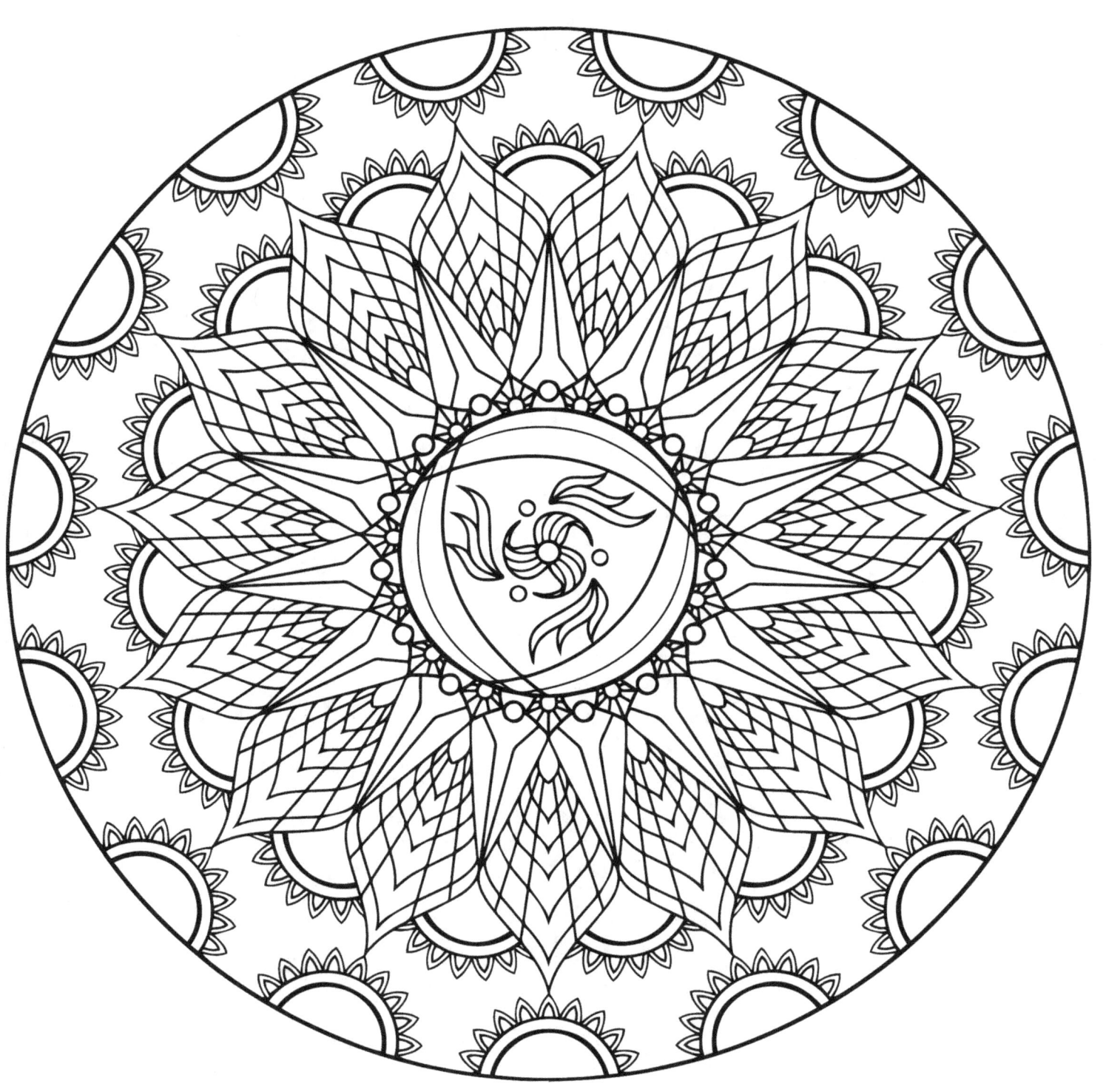

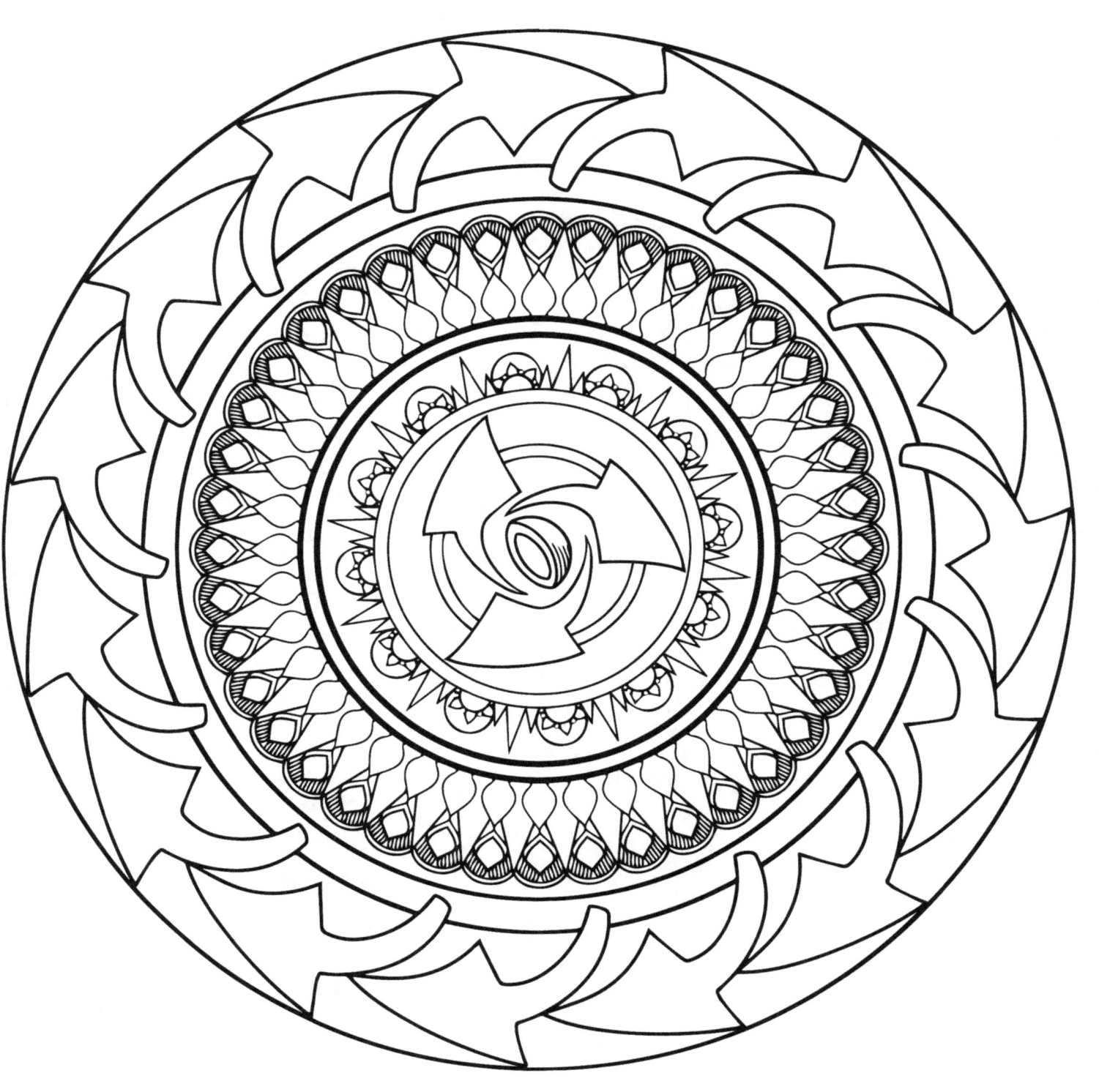

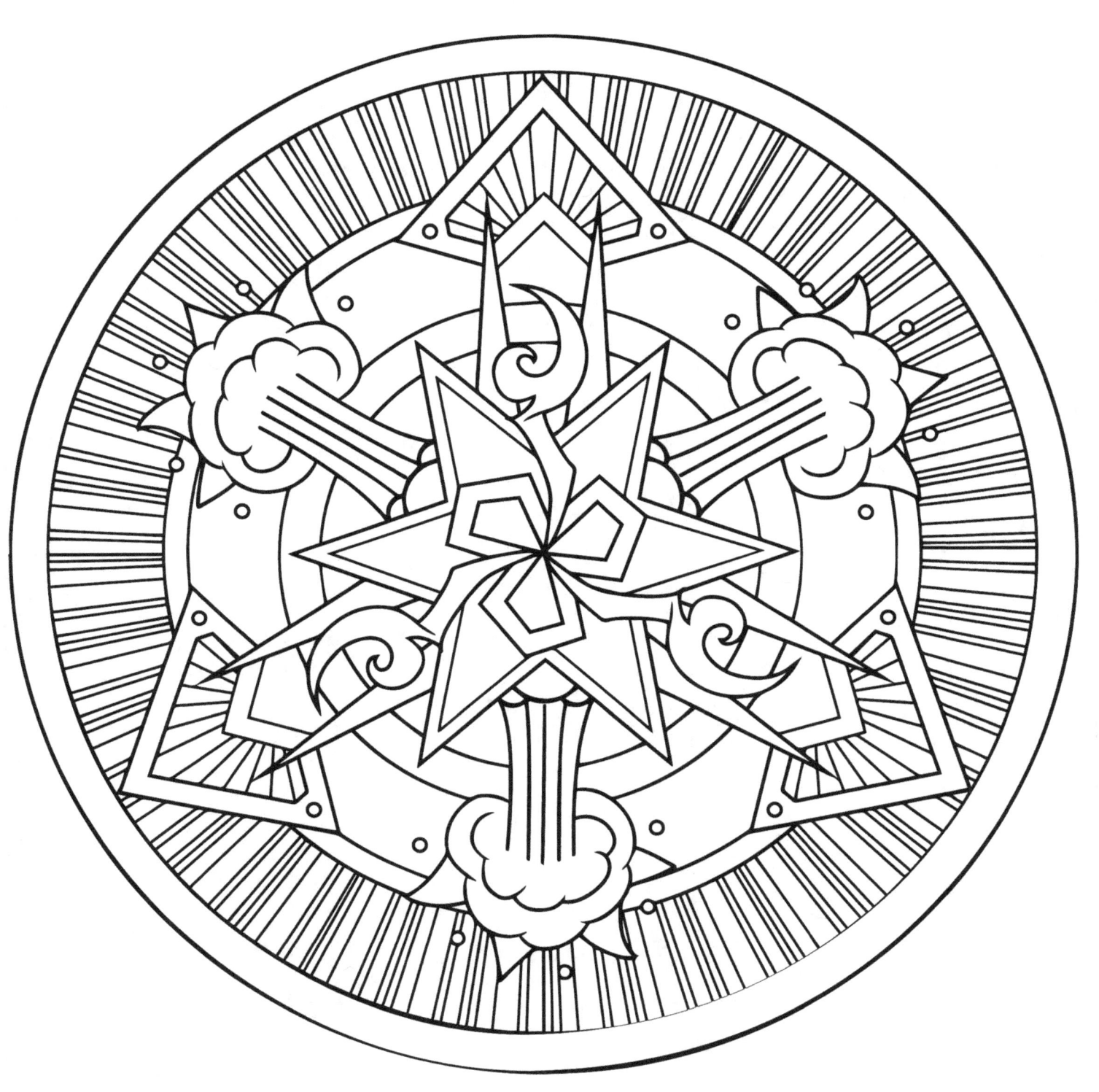

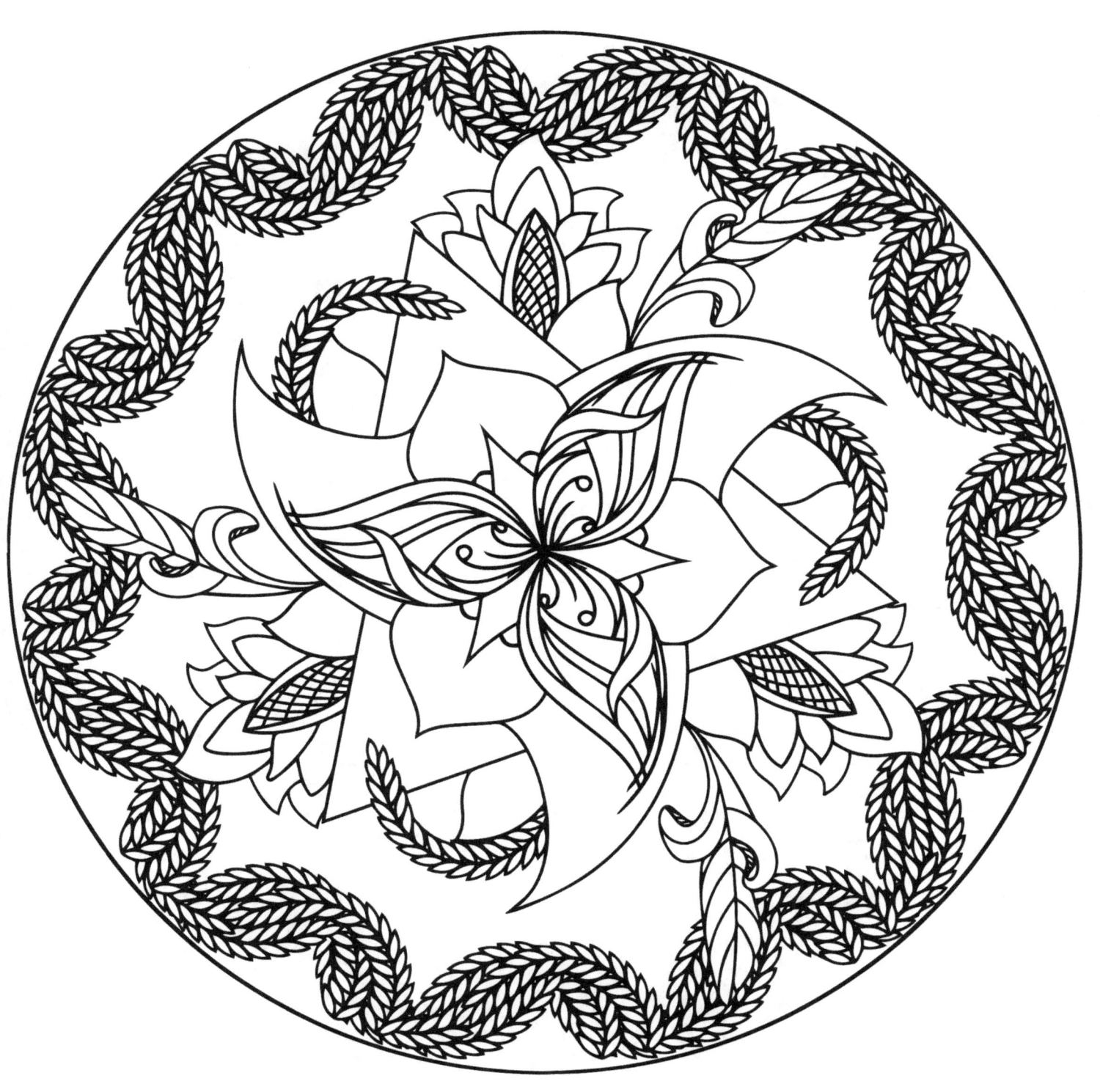

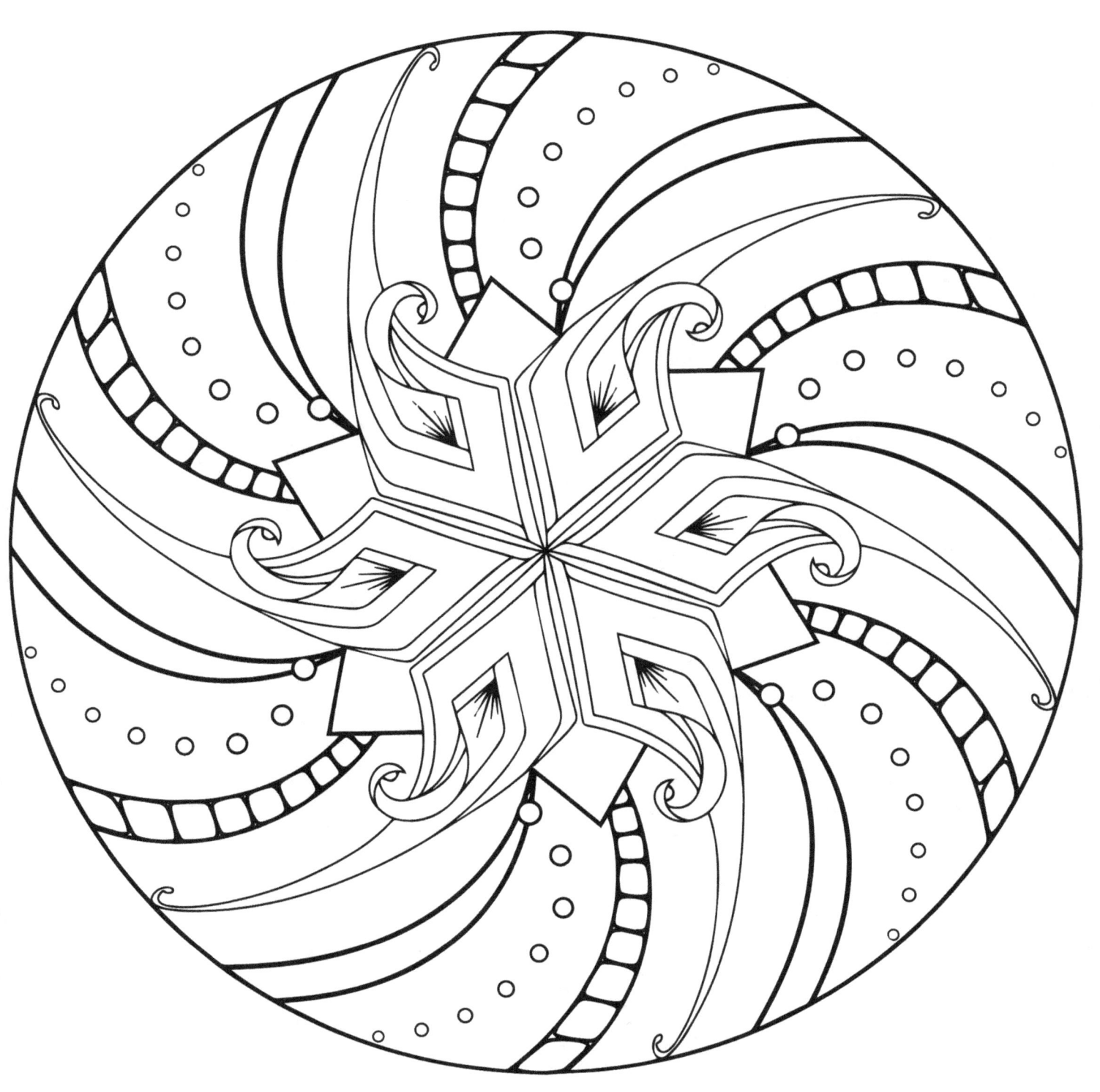

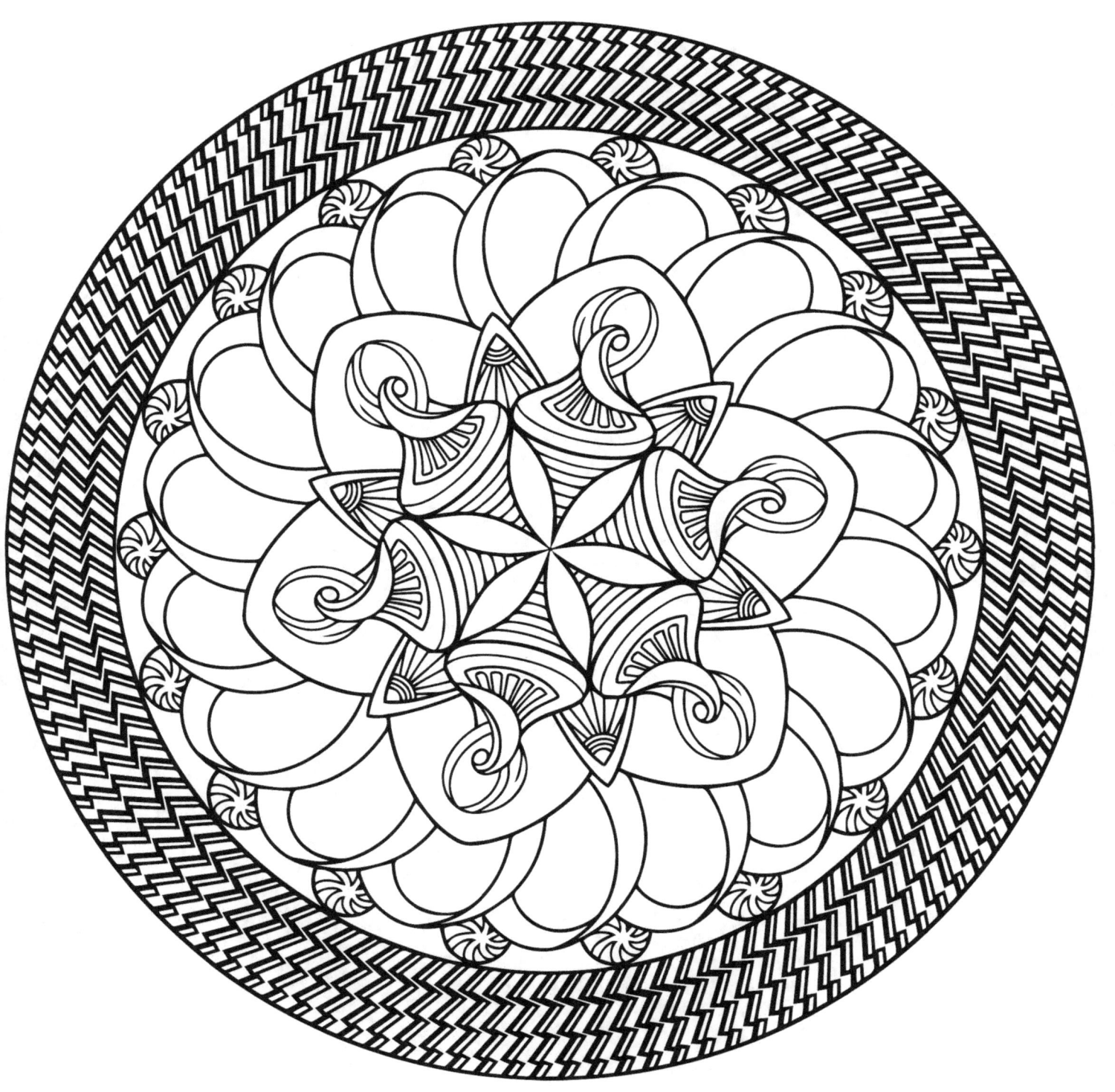

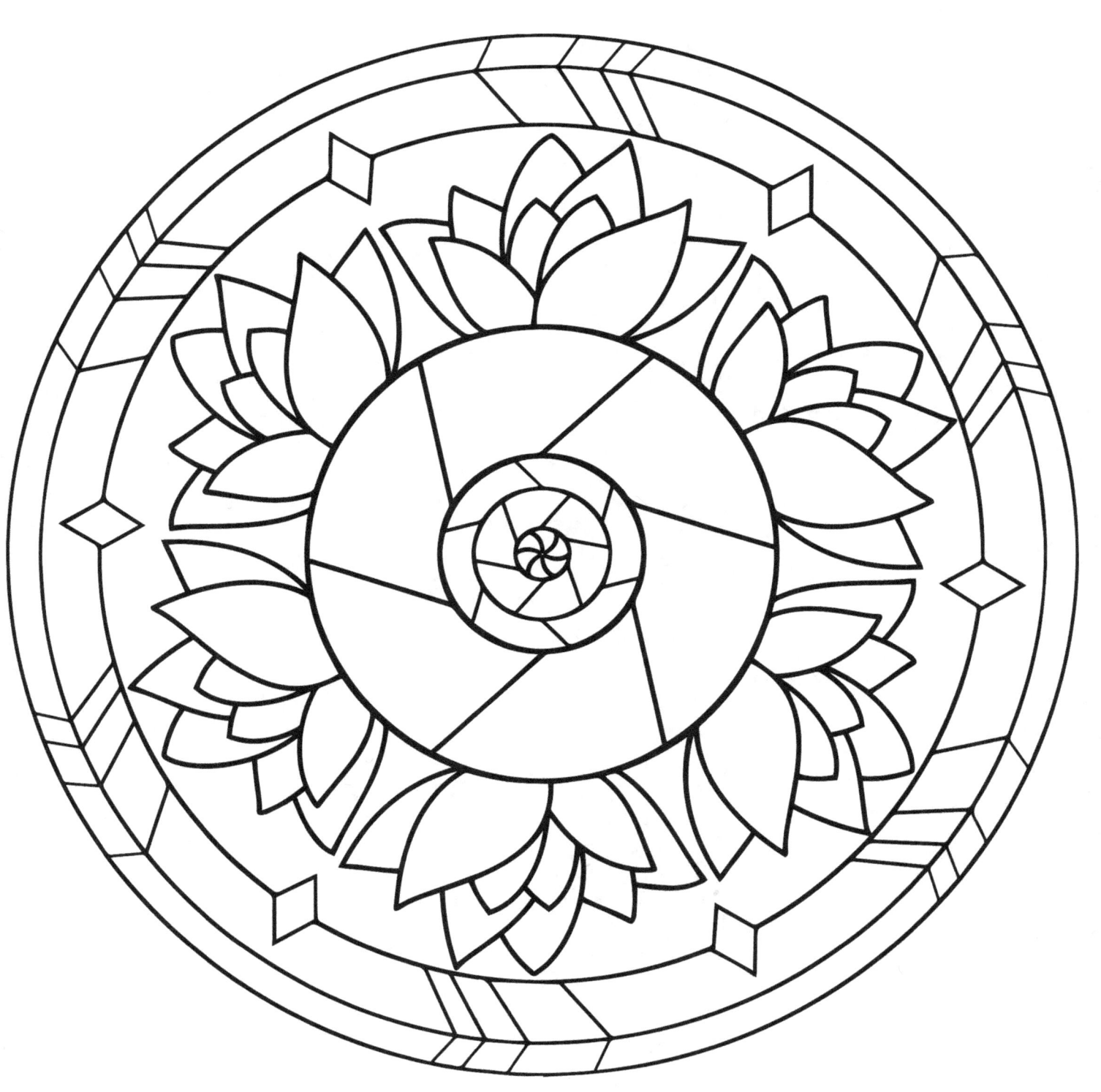

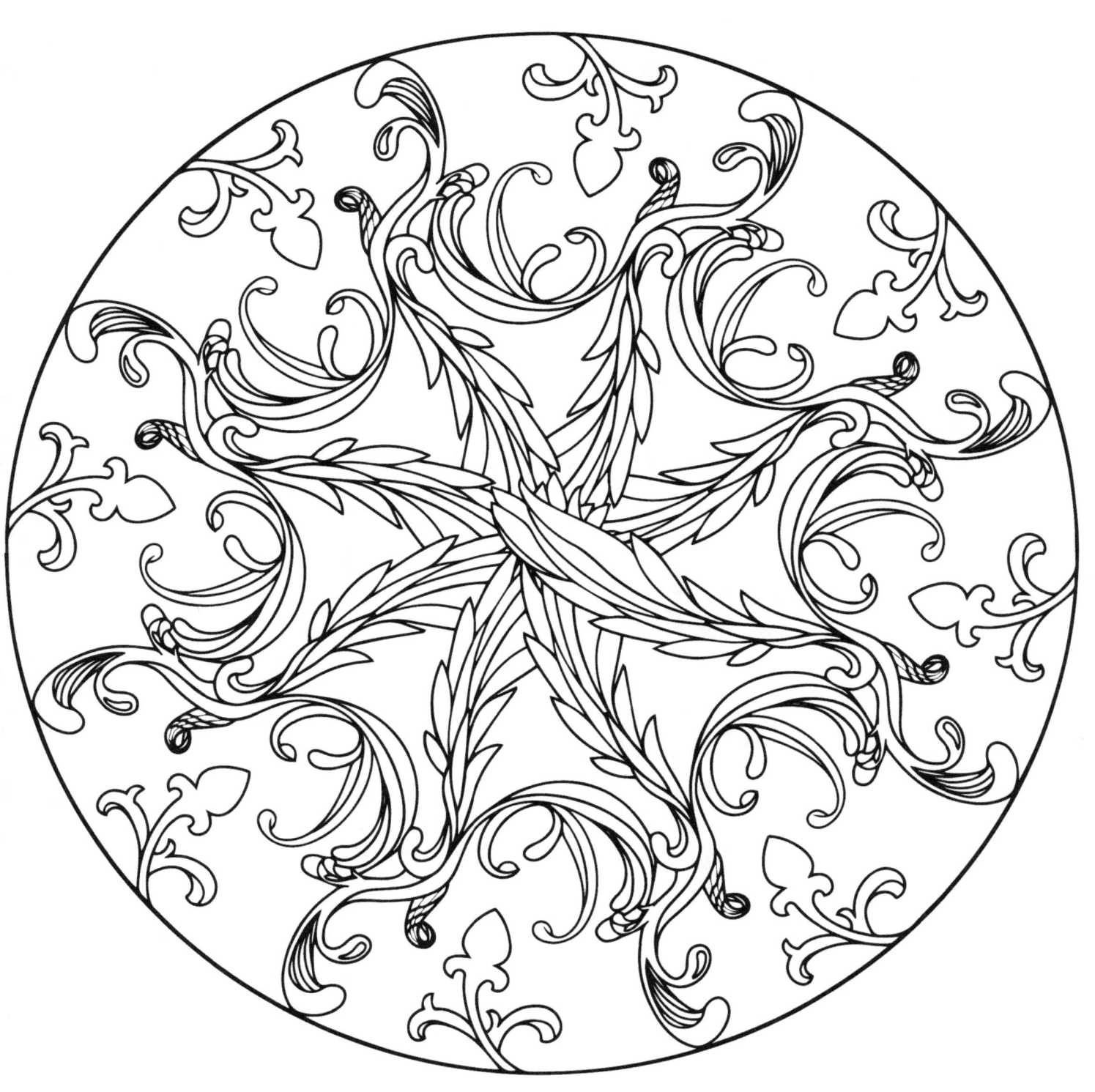

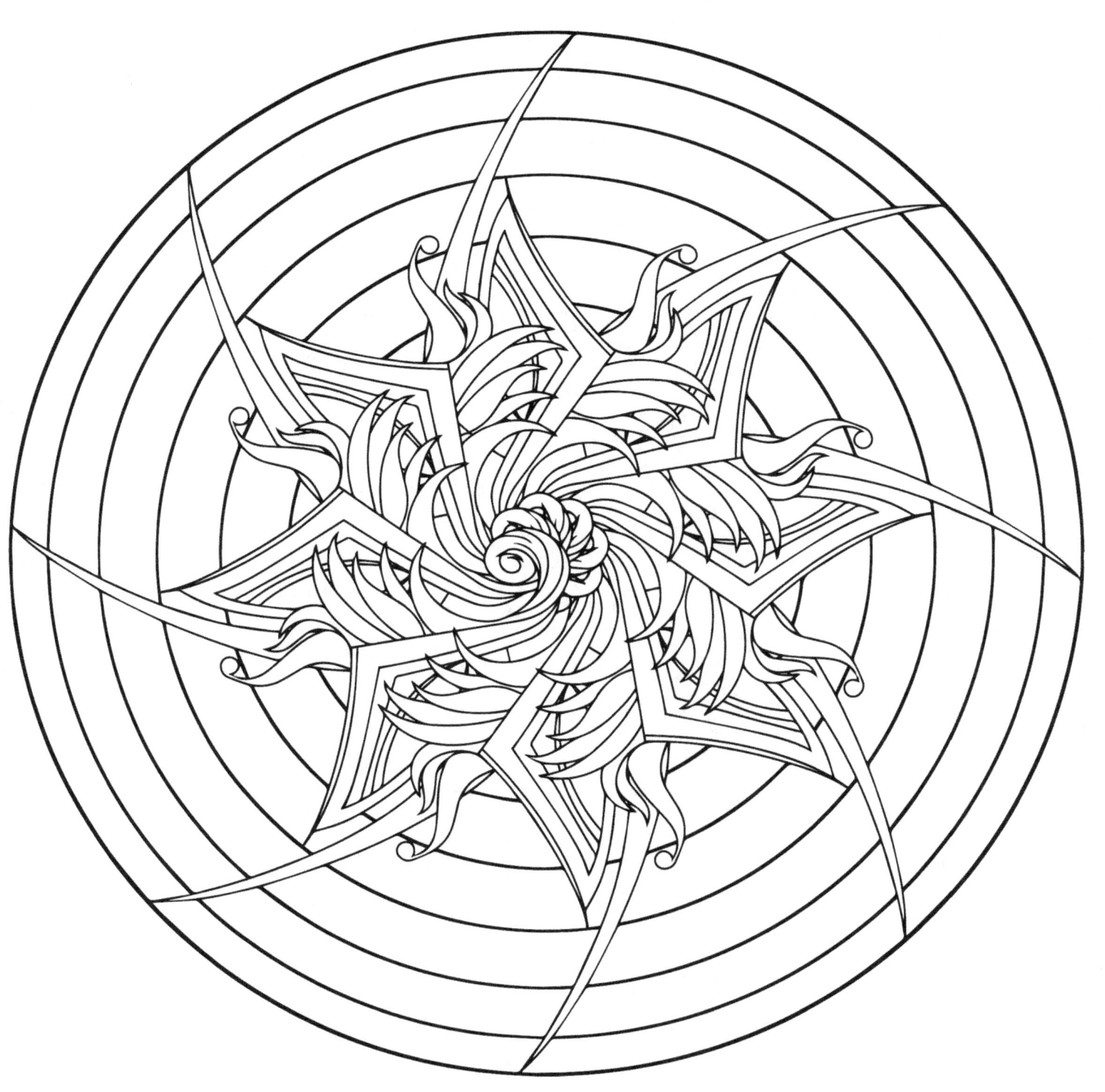

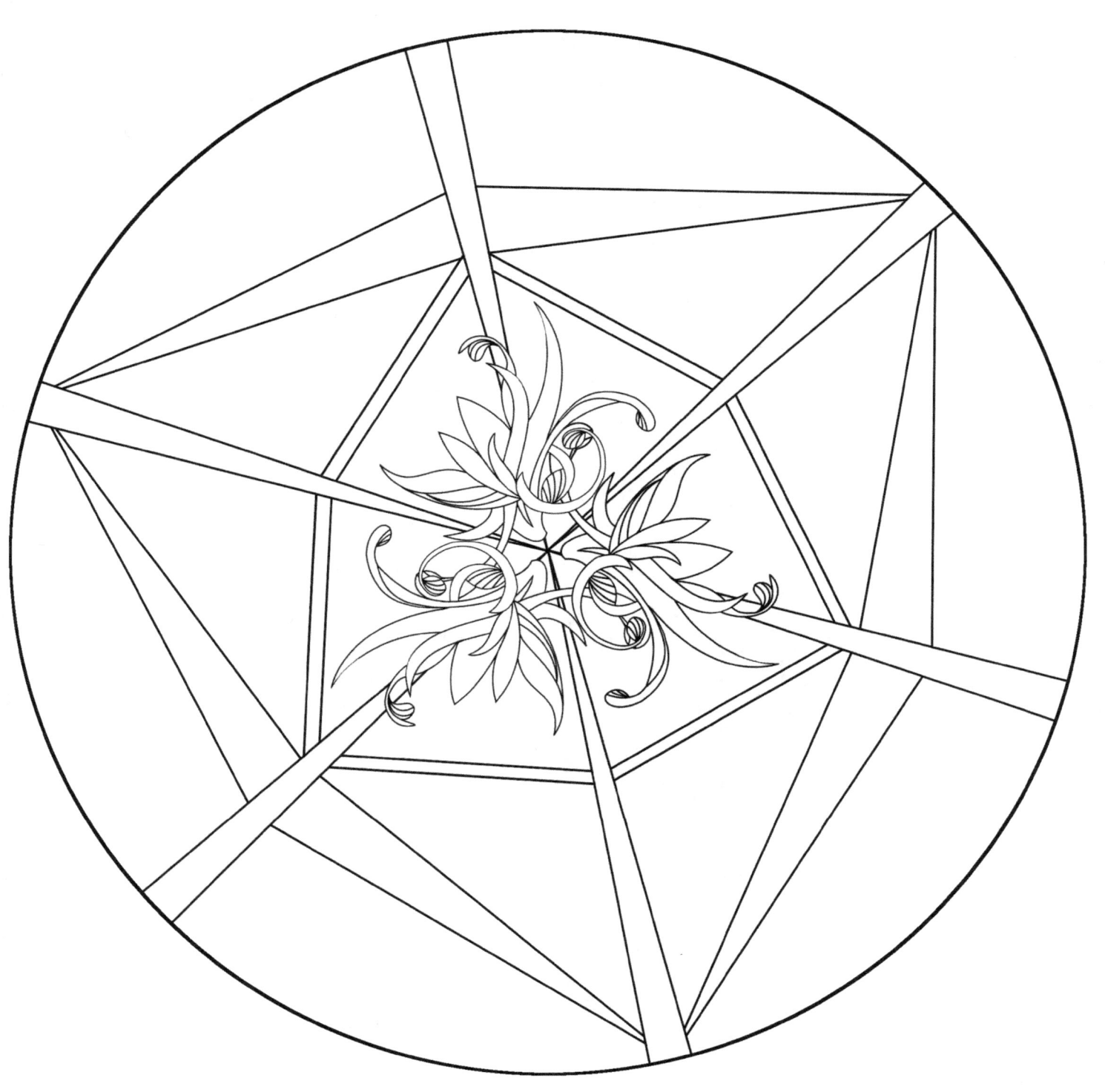

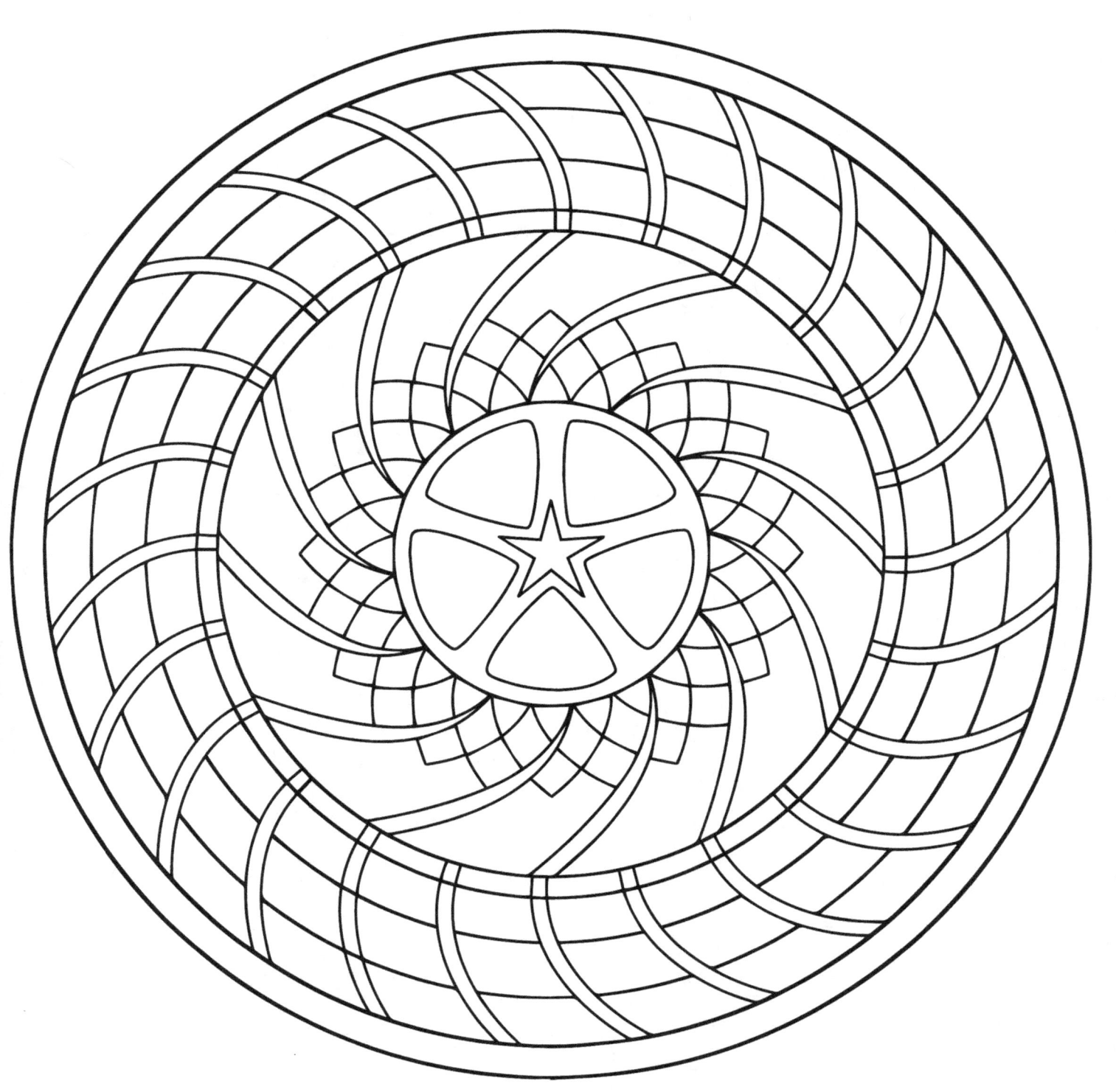

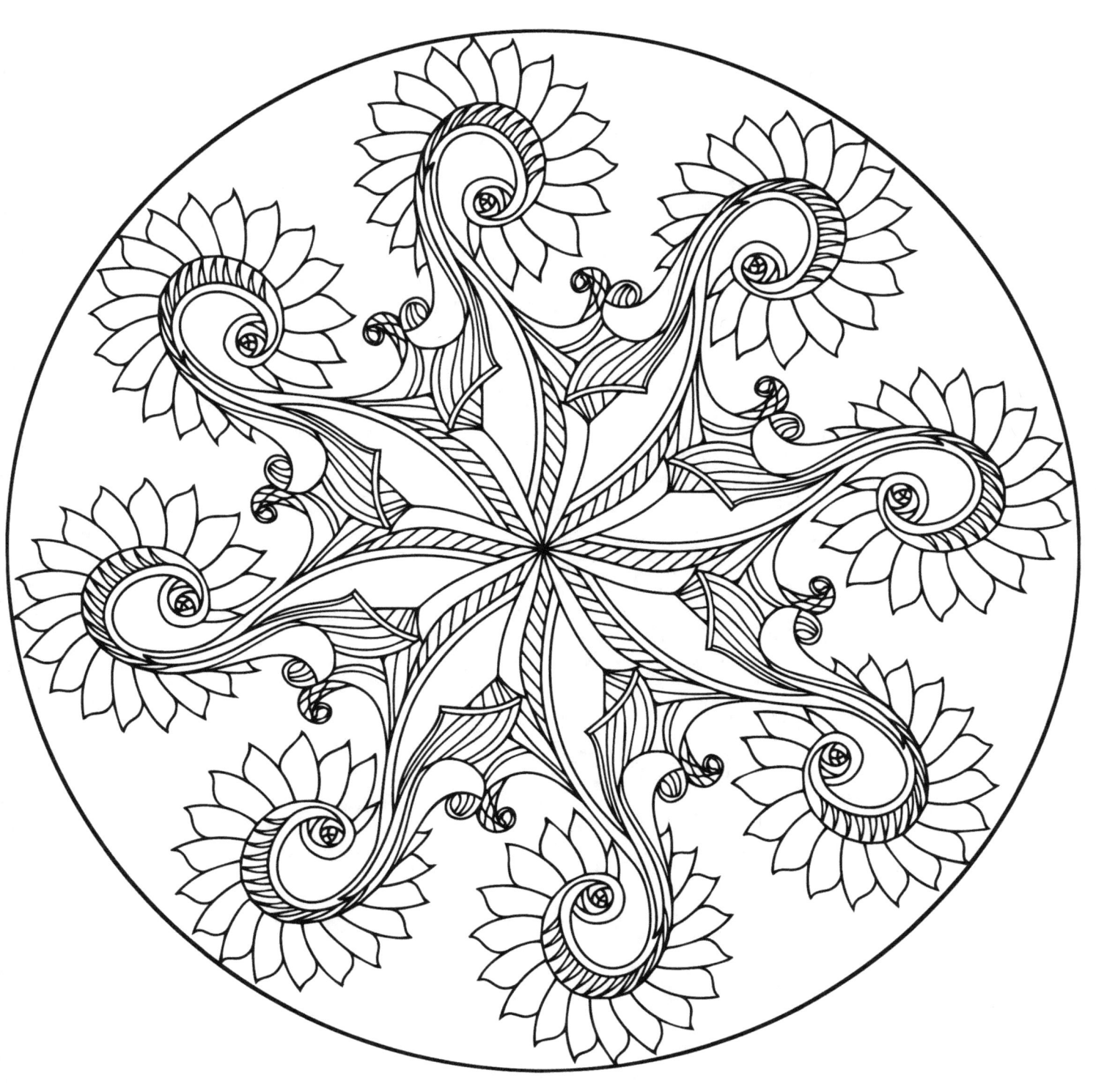

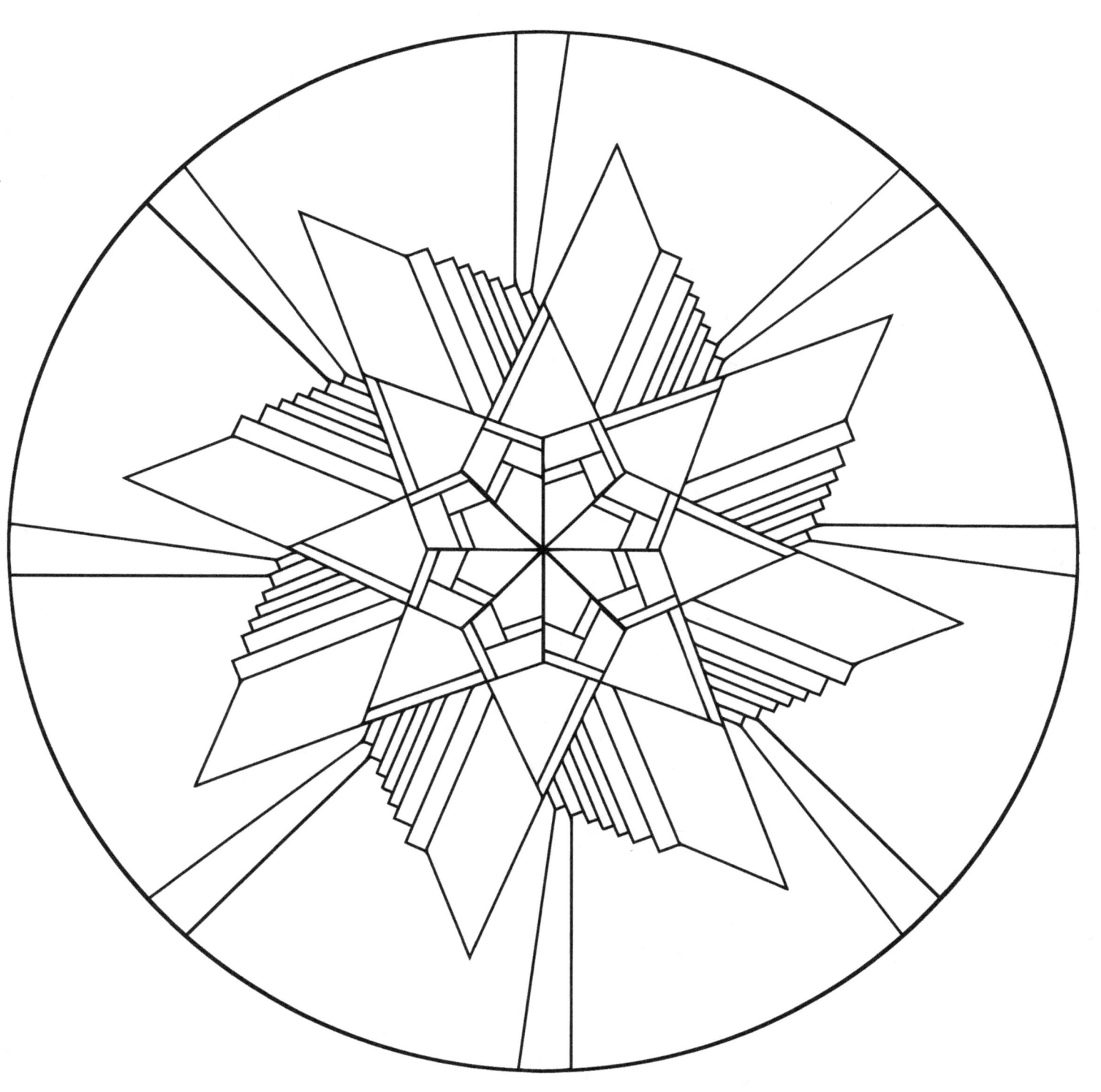

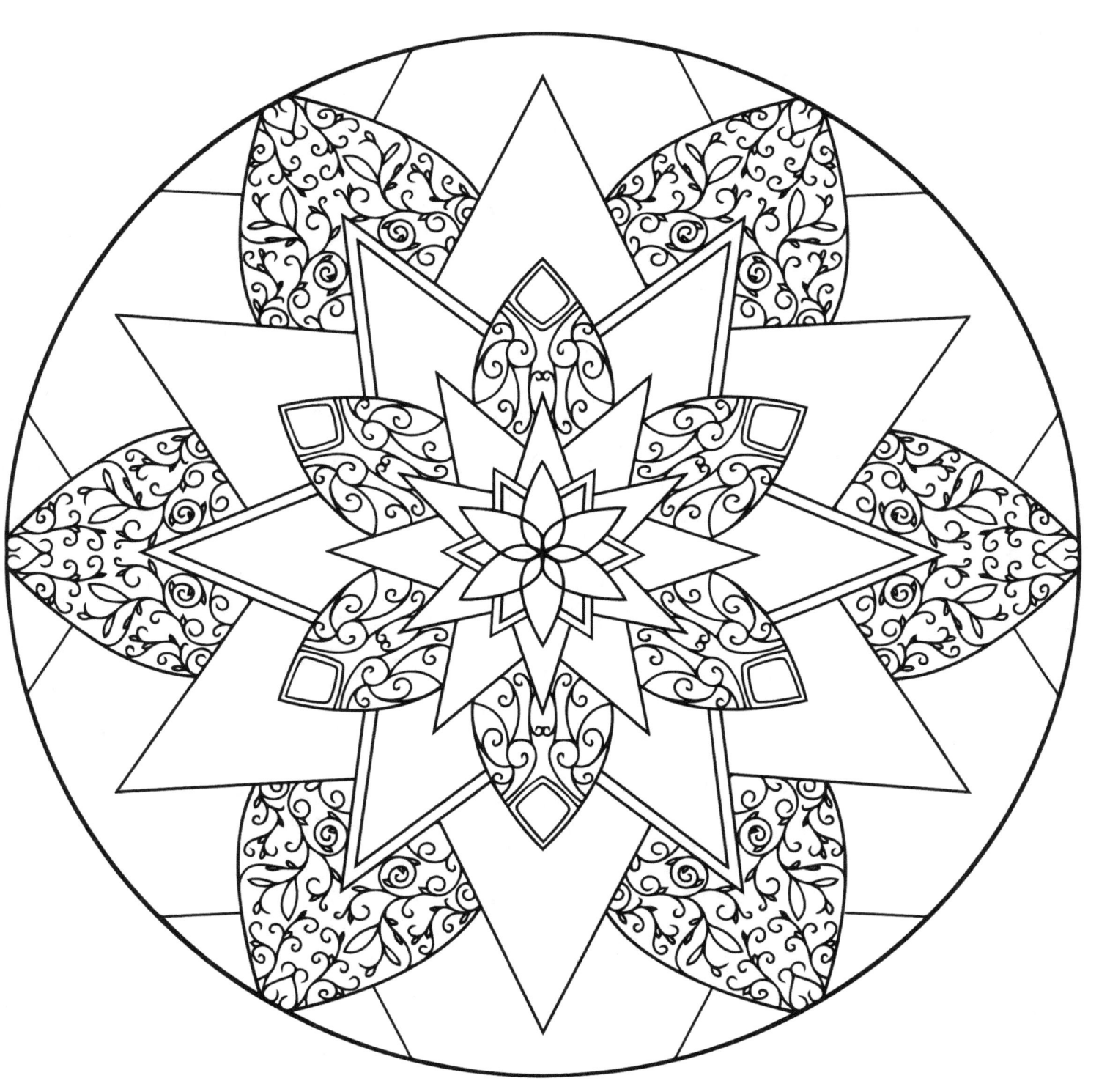

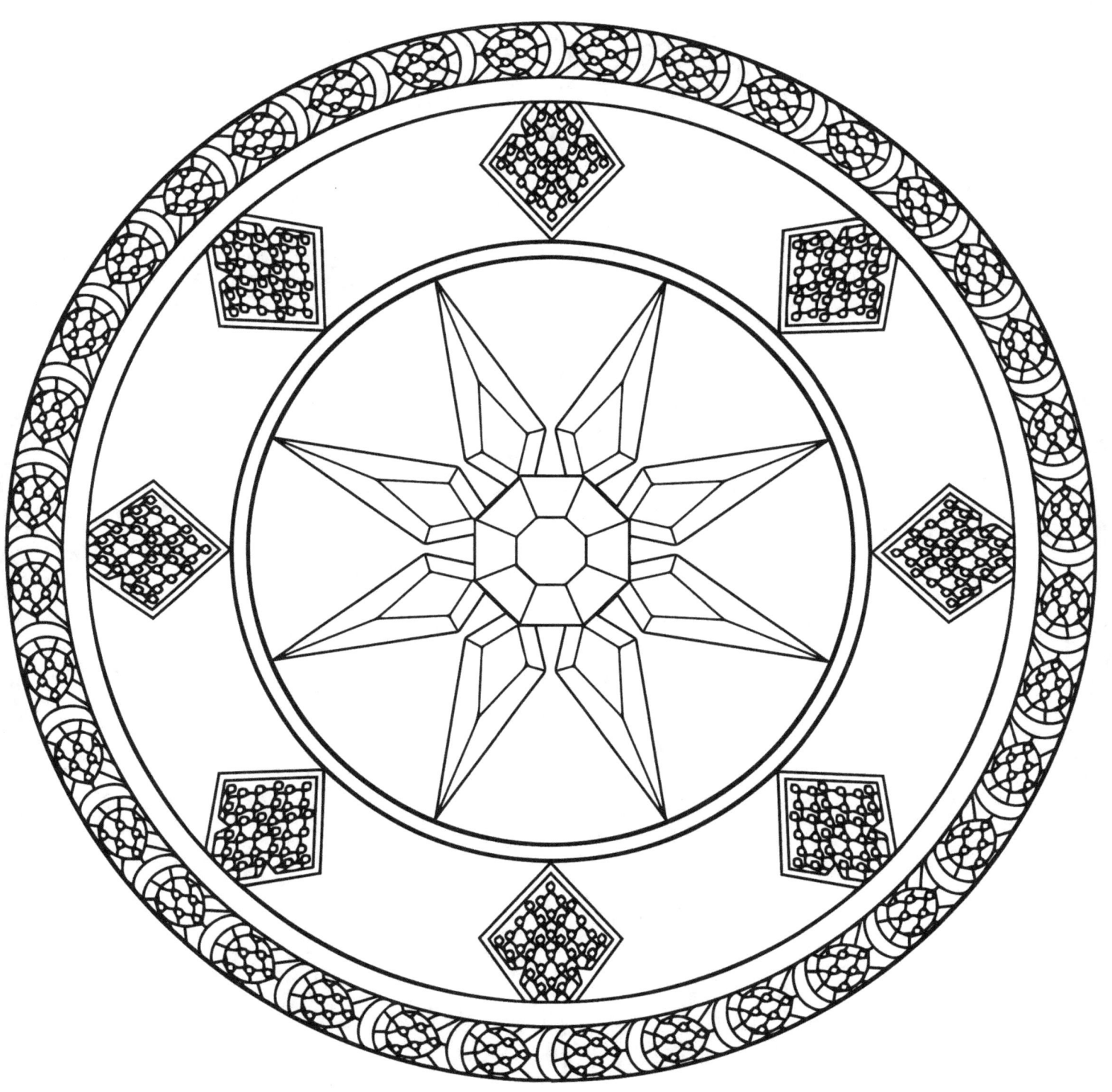

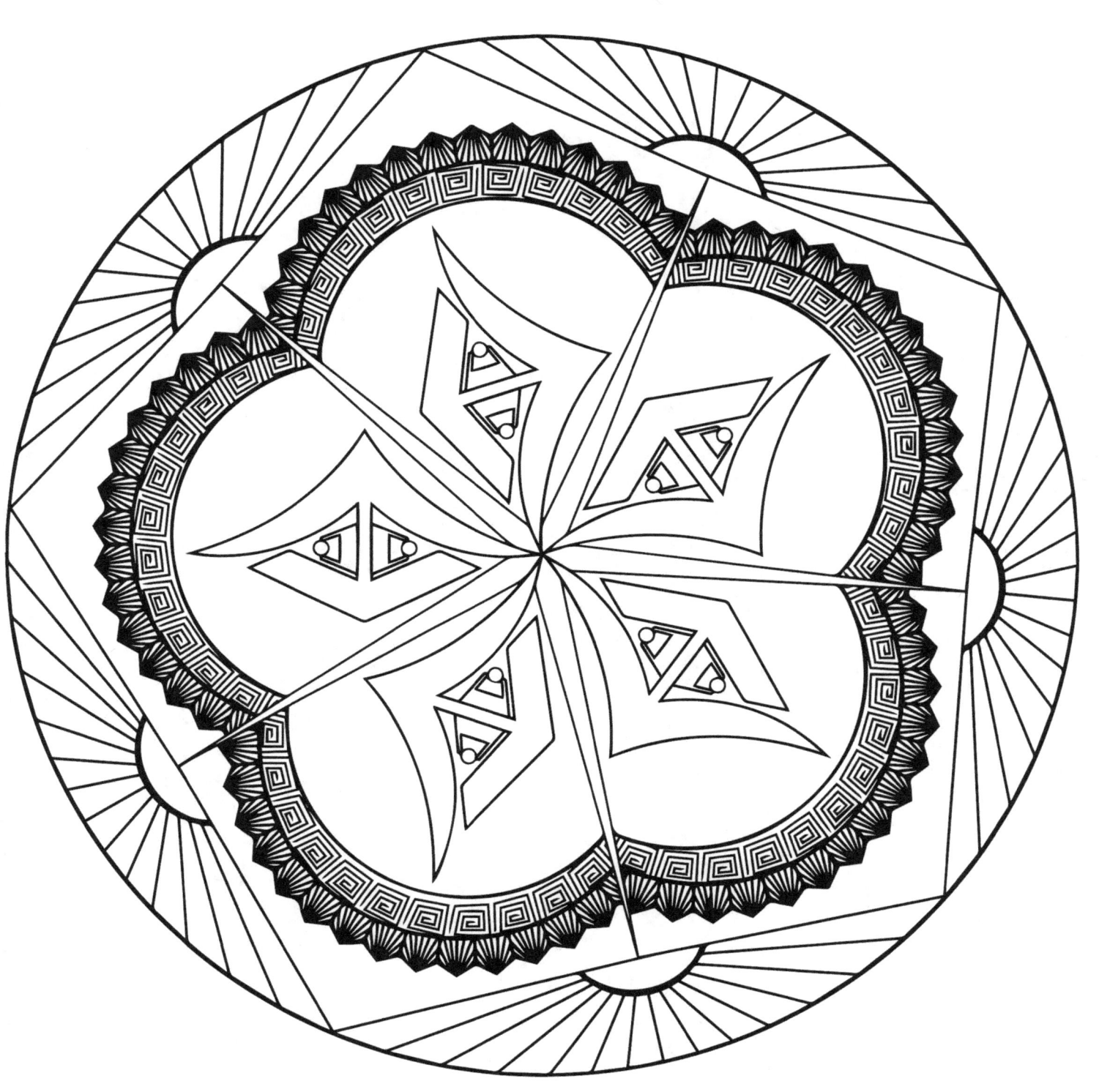

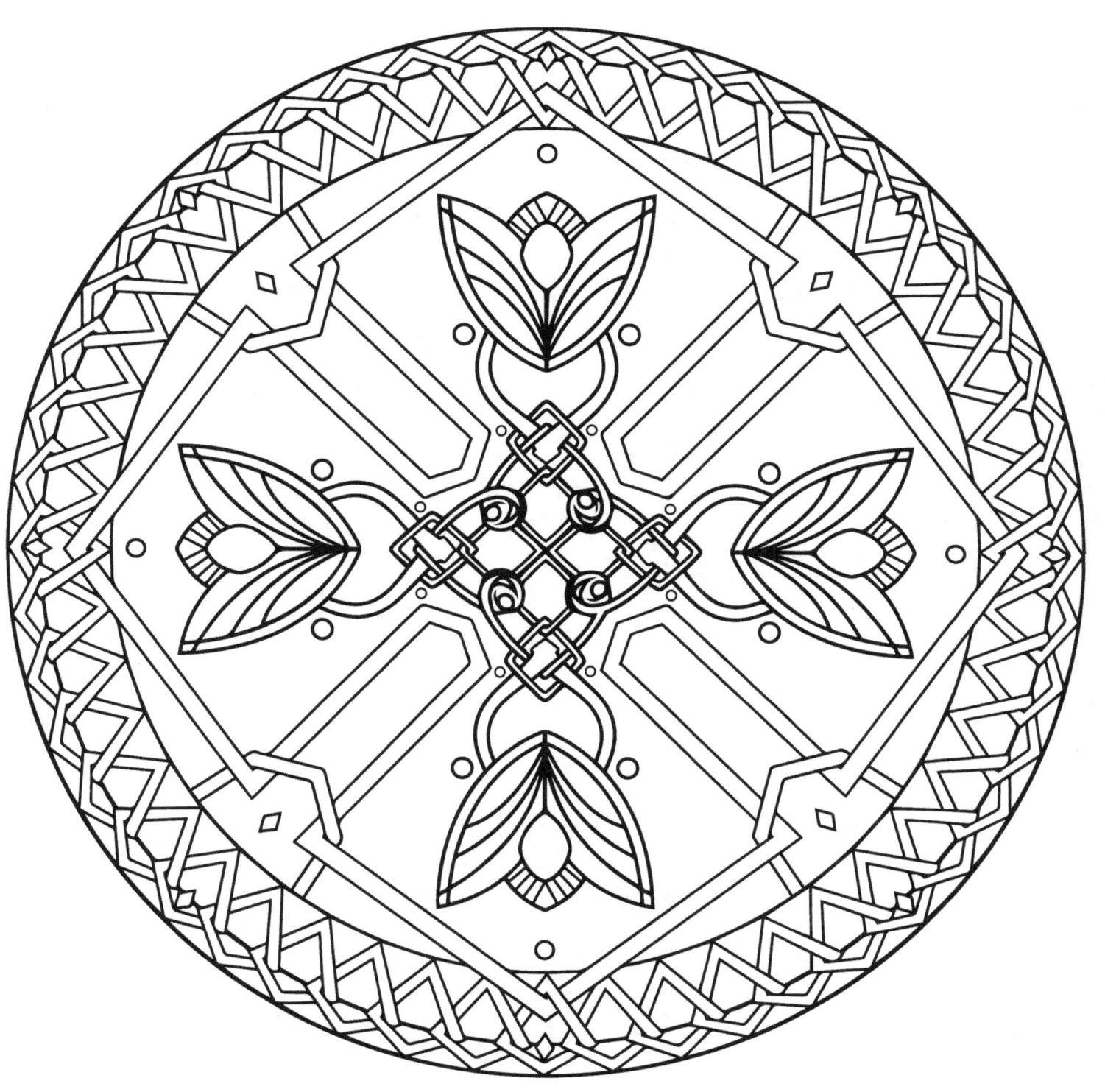

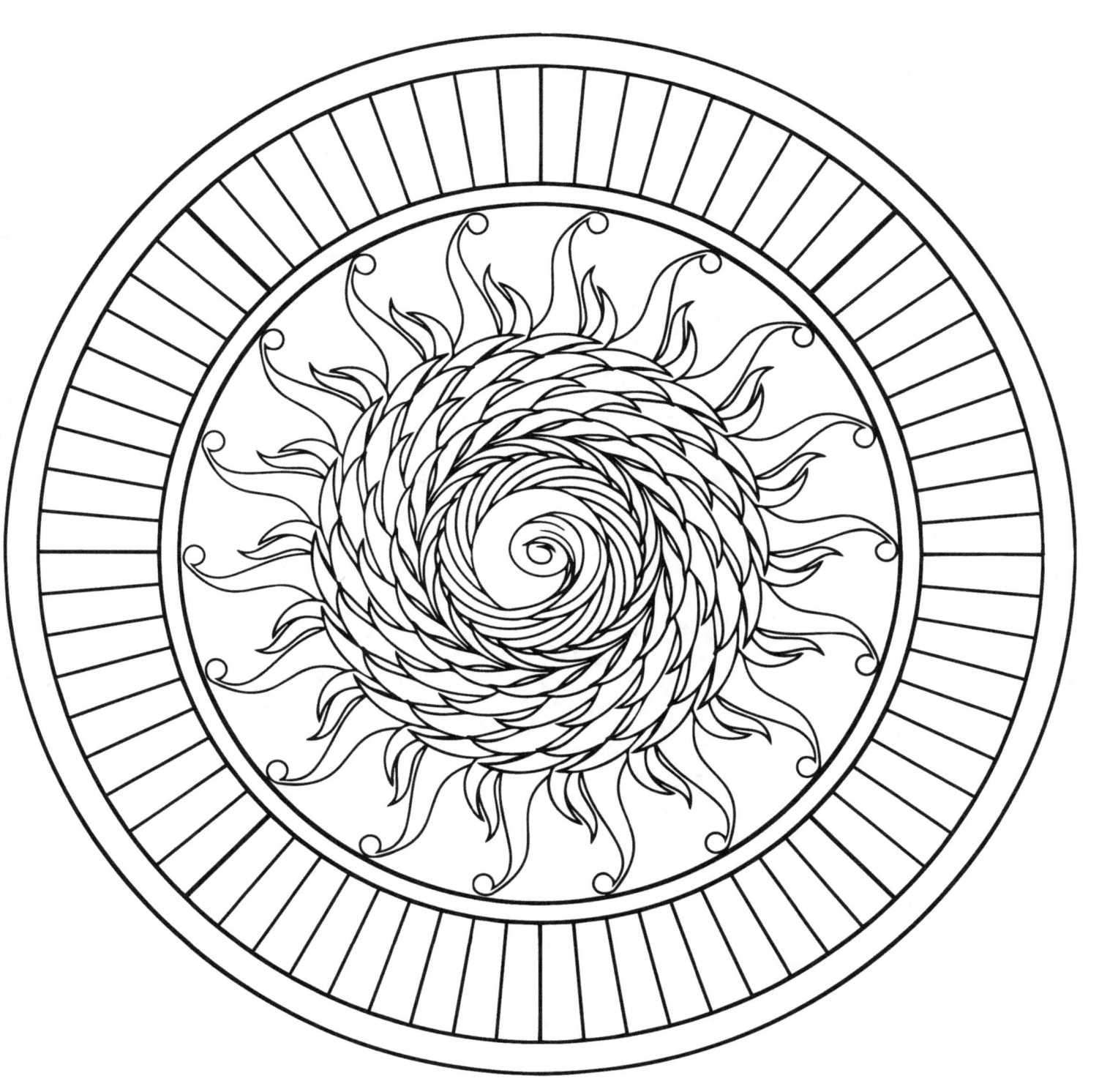

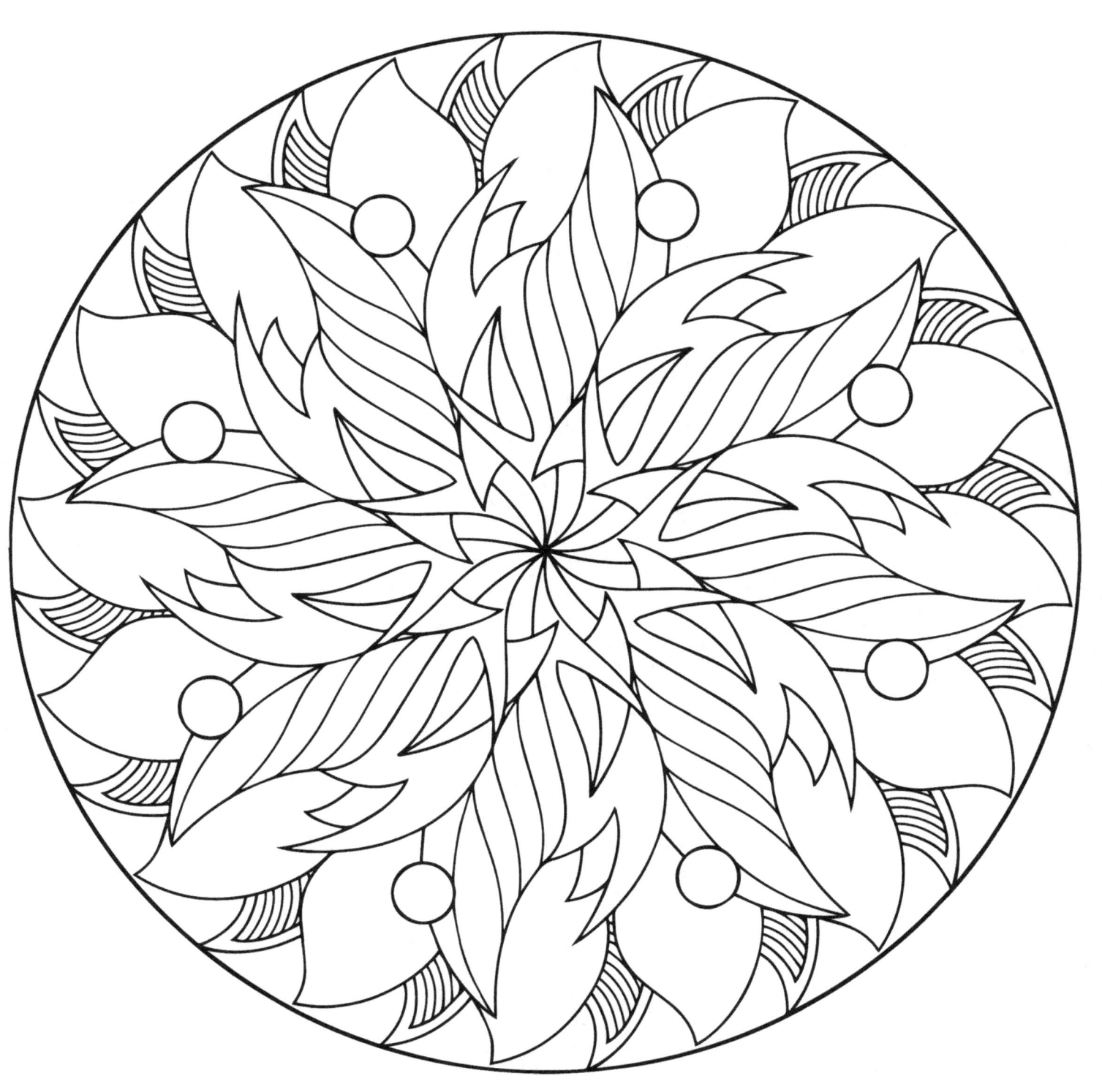

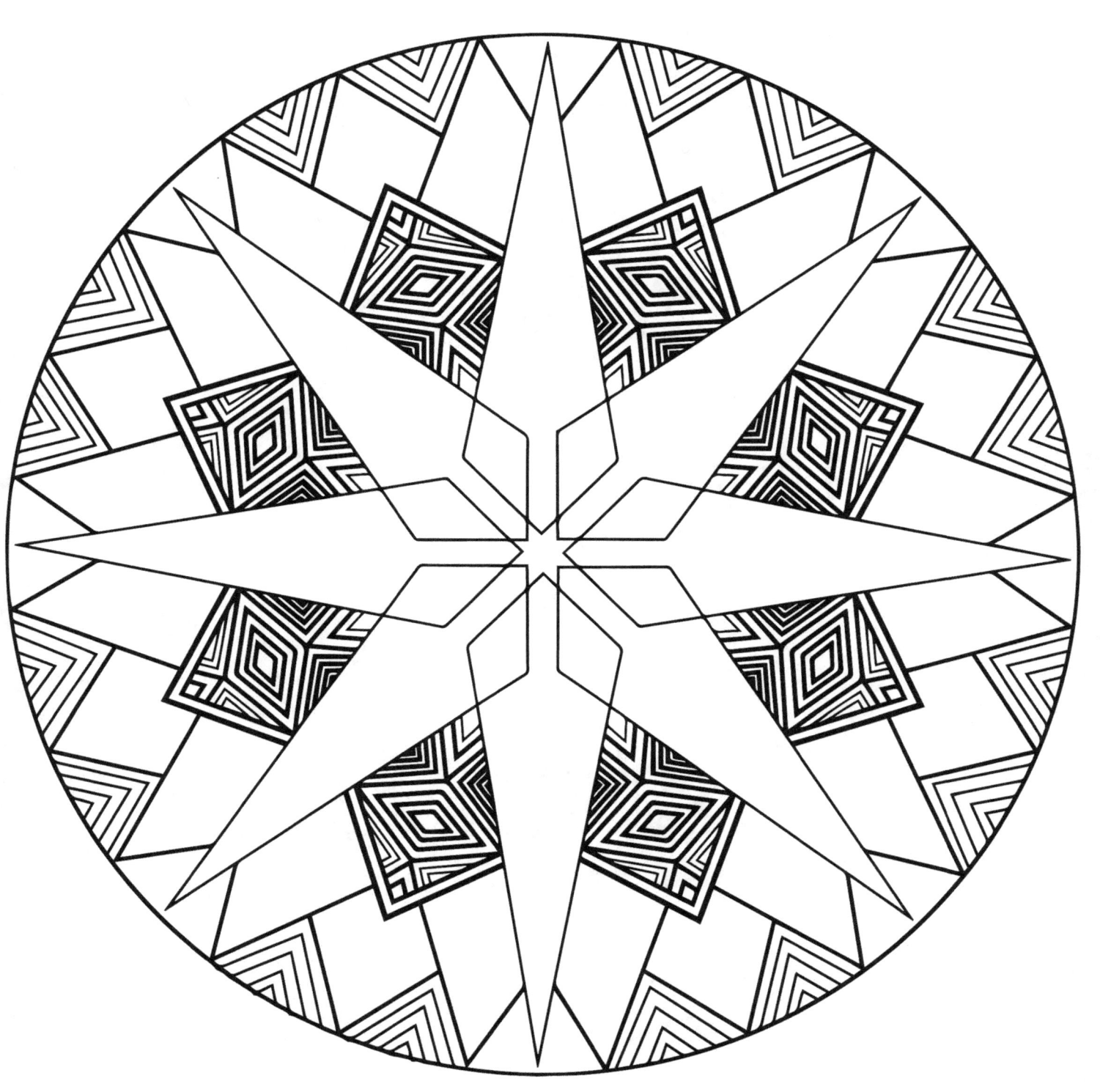

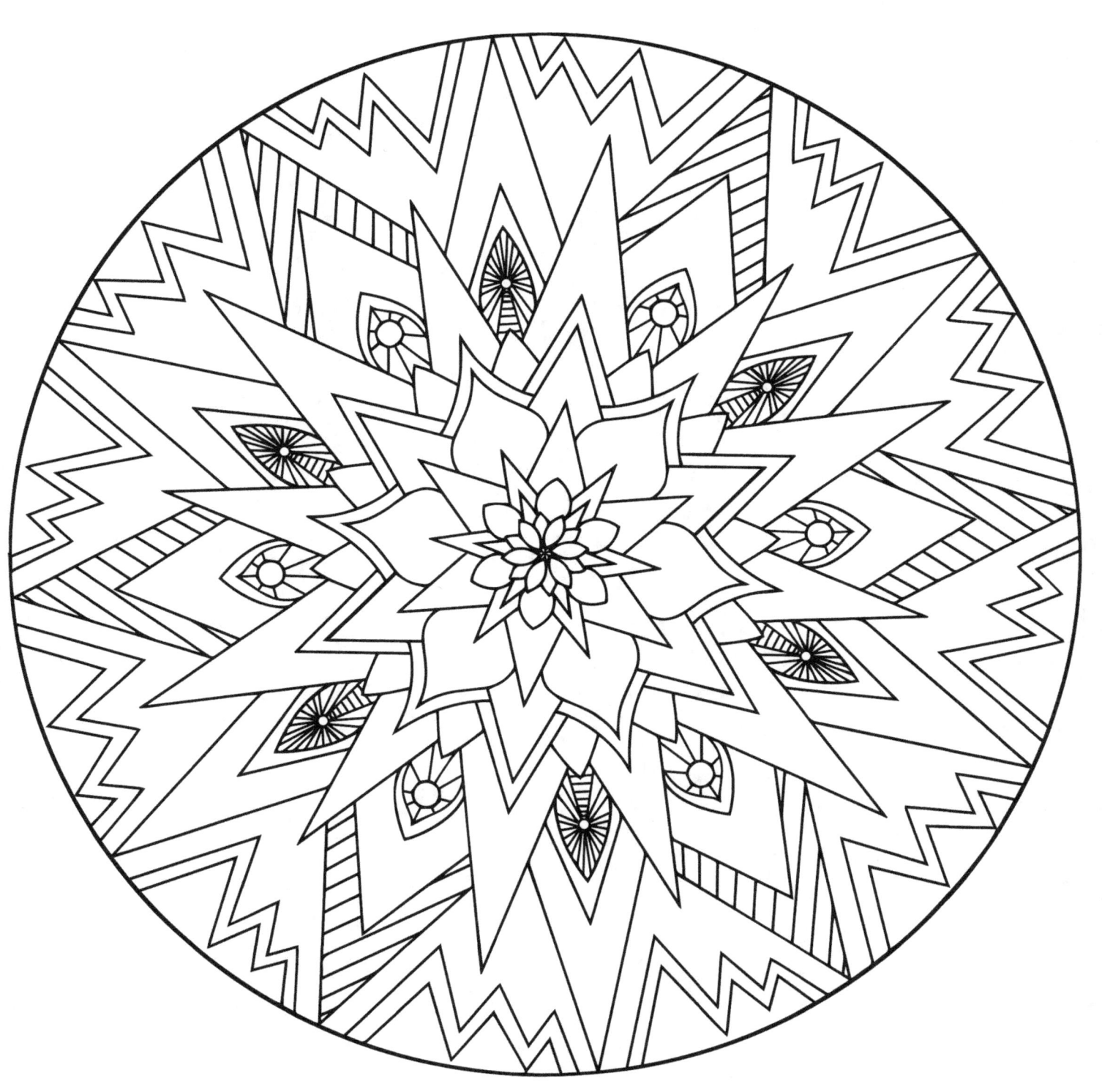

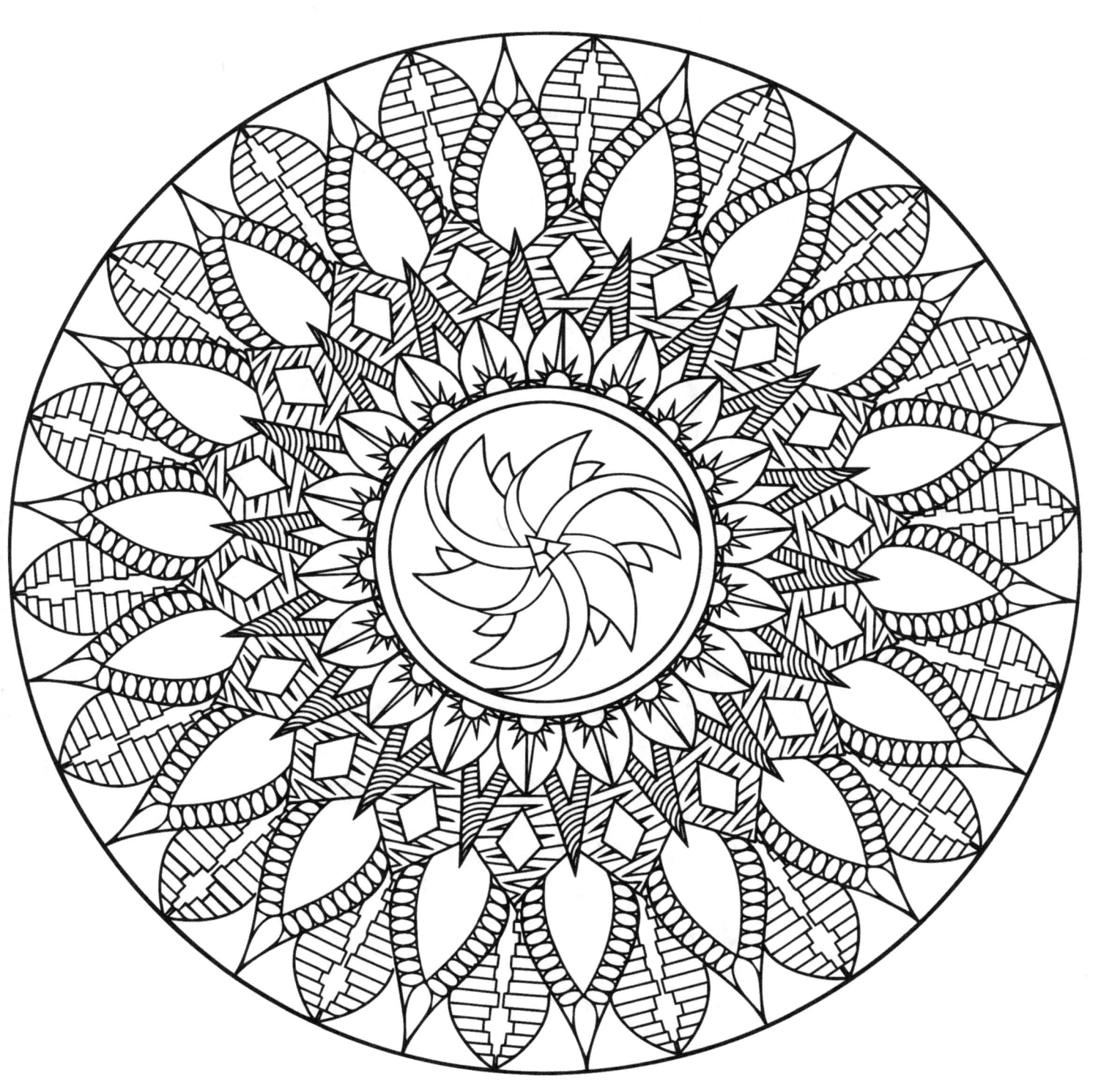

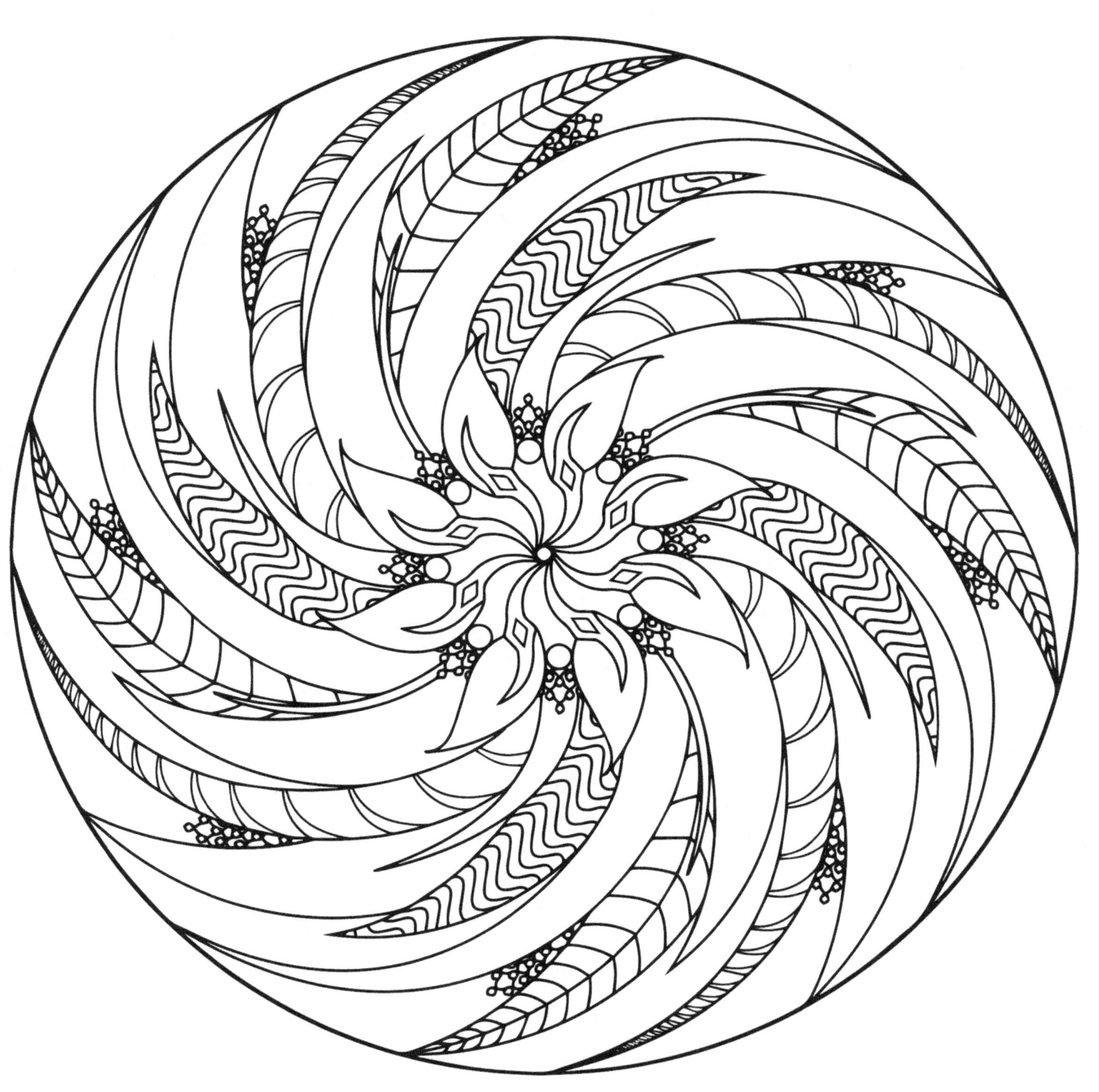